To our friend Buje

Peter Diel/Eric Menges

Surfing

In Search of the Perfect Wave

Meyer & Meyer Sport

Original title:
Surfing – Auf der Suche nach der perfekten Welle
– Aachen: Meyer und Meyer Verlag, 1999
(Adventure Sports)
Translated by James Beachus

British Library Cataloguing in Publication Data
A catalogue record for this book is available from the British Library

Diel/Menges:
Surfing – In search of the perfect wave/Diel/Menges. [Transl.: James Beachus].
– Oxford: Meyer & Meyer Sport (UK) Ltd., 2000
ISBN 1-84126-023-1

© 2000 by Meyer & Meyer Sport (UK) Ltd.
Oxford, Aachen, Olten (CH), Vienna, Québec
Lansing/Michigan, Adelaide, Auckland, Johannesburg, Budapest
Member of the World
Sportpublishers Association
Cover Photo: O'Neill, Bill Morris
Photos inside: Jeff Hornbaker, Quiksilver p. 8, 46, 157/
Joli p. 10, 70, 72, 104, 108, 132, 142, 149, 151, 154, 164, 168
Photo by Chiemsee, Xandi Kreuzeder p. 10, 53
Photo by Chiemsee, Eric Aeder p. 54, 58, 102, 111/
Roland Hansky p. 139/ Ecki Hillebrecht p. 82/ Tony King, Surf Travel Co. p. 31, 94, 161, 167
Kuta Lines Australia p. 99, 146/ Ineika p. 135
Menges/Diel p. 10, 12, 15, 16, 29, 40, 49, 52, 64, 66, 76, 118, 129
Photo by O'Neill, Bill Morris p. 14, 56, 88, 91, 96, 107, 113
Wave Tours p. 41/ Fanatic p. 115
Drawings: Stefan "Muli" Müller
Cover design: Birgit Engelen, Stolberg
Cover and Type exposure: frw, Reiner Wahlen, Aachen
Editorial: Dr. I. Jaeger, Aachen, John Coghlan
Typesetting: Quay
Printed and bound in Germany
by Druckpunkt Offset GmbH, Bergheim
ISBN 1-84126-023-1
e-mail: verlag@meyer-meyer-sports.com

CONTENTS

Page

Foreword 7

I. The Origin of Surfing 11

II. Surfing for Beginners 13

1	How to Start 13
1.1	Requirements 13
1.2	Equipment 15
1.2.1	The Right Surfboard for the Beginner 15
1.2.2	The Wetsuit 17
1.2.3	Wax and Leash 19
1.3	Preparation 21
2	The First Wave 23
2.1	The Right Waves for the Beginner 23
2.2	Get Ready (on the Beach) 26
2.3	How Do I Get out? 27
2.3.1	Entering the Water 28
2.3.2	Paddling 28
2.3.3	Dealing with Broken Waves 30
2.4	How Do I 'Catch' a Wave? 32
2.4.1	Paddling for a Wave 33
2.4.2	Catching a Wave 38
2.4.2.1	The Prone Position 38
2.4.2.2	Standing up 39
2.5	How Do I Get back to the Beach? 43
3	Now Let's Surf! 45
3.1	Riding a Wave 45
3.2	The First Manoeuvres 49
3.3	General Tips for the Beginner 57

III. Advanced Surfing **58**

1   What's Next? 58
1.1   Requirements for the Advanced Surfer 58
1.2   Equipment for the Advanced 61
1.3   The Surf Code...69
1.4   The Duck Dive 74

2   How Waves Are Created...76
2.1   Weather..77
2.2   How Do I Read the Surf Spot 82

3   Let's Get Serious! 89
3.1   Surfing Hollow Waves 89
3.2   Surfing Big Waves..97
3.3   Manoeuvres for the Advanced 107

4   General Tips for the Advanced 117

IV. Waves around the World **119**

1   Tips for a Surfari..119
2   Europe 126
3   USA and Hawaii...137
4   Australia 145
5   South Pacific...154
6   Indonesia, Mexico and the Rest of the World 159

V. Competitive Surfing, Surf Lingo and Information **169**

     Competitive Surfing..169
     Surf Lingo 171
     Information..175

Foreword

On a trip around the South Pacific, we were surfing together with a group of Australians on a remote reef in Fiji. During a wave lull, as we started chatting they asked where we came from. The answer, "... from Europe" caused a few frowned looks, and we could see word balloons with big question marks appearing over the heads of the Australians – "do you guys have any waves?"

Of course, for most people living in Europe (like us – the authors), surfing is rather an unusual sport, and there have been many occasions when it has been necessary to start explaining what surfing is all about. "No, not surfing the Internet, (whoever thought up this term should be punished anyway), no we do not use a sail. Yes, exactly that – riding the waves – just like in Hawaii."

On top of all that, here we are, two Euros, writing a book about surfing. However, we are confident that the experience we have gathered during a long learning process, will be of some use to surfers and to beginners, who have not grown up by the sea or live there. Indeed, it does require particular effort and, above all, regular travel to become a surfer. But the message we give you is that anyone can learn surfing and have lots of fun doing it.

People are continually discovering this fascinating sport. Although snowboarding (surfing on snow) and skateboarding (surfing on the road) originally evolved as alternatives for surfing, there are today many skate- and snowboarders, who are still only just now discovering surfing as a sport. The characteristics of these sports are very similar and many of the movement sequences resemble each other.

There is the unforgettable and unbelievable kick when you snowboard through fresh powder, get air in a half pipe, or successfully come out of a tube on a wave.

Kelly Slater, World Champion 1992/94/95/96/97/98 (Photo: Jeff Hornbaker, Quiksilver)

We have been surfing for about 15 years and have taught many of our friends how to surf. "Just do it!" – is the correct approach to all this as far as surfing is concerned. Experience has shown, however, that a considerable amount of time, hassle and injury can be saved if some theoretical knowledge is gained beforehand. Well, you guessed it. Now is the moment to invest some time and read about the basics of wave riding. We do not want to teach you technically laid out methods. On the contrary, we would like to offer some theory, and rather more so, use a few anecdotes and stories from the surfing world to explain what it is all about. This book has been written with the beginner as well as the advanced in mind. The beginner will not have to continually pester the "cool surfer" with simple questions such as "Why do you tie that rope to your foot?" He will not ever again make the whole beach erupt in laughter by waxing the wrong side of the surfboard (the underside). Also the advanced surfer will find some tips in our book that will help him on his way to becoming a genuine hardcore surfer.

A few years ago we decided to realise our greatest dream - a journey round the world in search of the perfect wave. Our journey took us from Bali to Australia, New Zealand, Fiji, Tahiti, USA and to Mexico. Believe us - there is the perfect wave. One will never surf the same wave twice because every wave is different to the next. To make the search a little easier, our book includes details of various surfing destinations in this world. Some tips will serve to help and ensure that you have fun on a surftrip in unfamiliar countries and waters. A famous surfer once answered the question on who was the best surfer in the world by replying, "The best surfer in the world is the one having the most fun." But, careful, riding waves is addictive! If you have surfed once, then you will soon have nothing but waves swirling around in your brain. Along these lines – "Surf hard and respect the ocean." Enjoy reading this book!

N.B. To avoid repetition and easier reading; whenever the male pronoun is used the female form is equally meant to be included.

*Surfing on the road, on water and on snow
(Photos: Street – Menges, Diel; Water – Joli; Snow - by permission of Chiemsee, photographer
Xandi Kreuzeder)*

I. THE ORIGIN OF SURFING

*E*ven today the Hawaiians and the Tahitians still argue over the origin of surfing. One thing is sure – it started in Polynesia. Just when surfing started there, however, is still a little uncertain and not proven. There are indications in their native songs that this spectacular water sport was already being carried out in the 15th century.

So, even before the white man placed foot on the Polynesian shores, the waves were being ridden there. On his sea travels in 1777, Captain James Cook was the first white man to enjoy watching the natives playing with the waves.

Thanks to one of their successors, the Hawaiian Duke Kahanamoku, surfing became so popular in our time. Duke was an excellent swimmer and won several Olympic gold medals for the USA. On a visit to Australia, the "Duke" also demonstrated what he was capable of when it came to using a board. Riding waves – surfing – has become increasingly popular from that moment and has spread across to California, New Zealand, South Africa and to Europe.

There are, of course, many more legendary surfers who we should name here, like for example the American Greg Noll, "da Bull" – the big wave legend, or the second to none Australian Mark Richards – who won four consecutive world titles.

Then there is Nat Young – the Australian surfing legend, as well as the unbeatable, six times world Champion Kelly Slater – who is writing surfing history as you read this, and so on and so forth. But we want to tell you about surfing not history, so let's get on with it.

In the beginning was the wave (Photo: Menges/Diel)

II. SURFING FOR BEGINNERS

ow you know where wave riding comes from. But how are you going to turn yourself into a second Duke? Well, nothing is guaranteed, but the following sections will help for sure.

1   How to Start

o you have decided to become a surfer. Sounds good. Just think of all those unreal pictures on television and on videos! Looks really cool! But, unfortunately, it is not as easy as many top surfers make it look. The multitude of different factors that make it possible to glide on a wave, without a sail and without footstraps, turn the first steps into an uphill struggle.

As a word of encouragement, although many hours will be spent sitting in freezing water waiting for the waves that did not come and despair will sink in, all of a sudden it will all come together. The right wave, the correct paddling speed, no one in the way - and there you are - standing, surfing your first wave. What a feeling. So do not ever let yourself be discouraged. It is worth it.

1.1   Requirements

ho can learn to surf? Basically anyone who can swim. For surfing, the size of the body is relatively insignificant. Actually, short surfers have a little advantage because of their lower centre of mass. Although men mainly carry out this sport, women can easily learn to surf. Irrespective whether you are a man or a woman you must have a lot of patience and endurance. Surfing demands skill, timing and knowledge about waves, currents and the sea bottom.

That is you (in a few years)
(Photo: O'Neill, photographer: Bill Morris)

Surfing can sometimes be a little dangerous, but if you are well-prepared, you can recognise your own physical and psychological limits, even as a beginner you can have a lot of fun.

Oh yes, and another thing. You better start saving money for a surfing trip to Australia, Bali or Hawaii.

Anyone can learn to surf (Ineika Surfing School on Fuerteventura Photo: Menges/Diel)

1.2 Equipment
1.2.1 The Right Surfboard for the Beginner

*T*he selection of the right surfboard is important to get the right fun out of surfing, if you are a beginner or an advanced surfer. The first surfboard should be long, thick and wide. The length and thickness gives the board more buoyancy, which aids easier paddling, which lets you catch a wave more easily. The width gives the advantage of stability when standing up. Either a longboard, or a hybrid or so called Mini-Malibu is the most suitable board for the beginner. A typical longboard is between 9 and 10 foot long, 22 inches wide and between 3-4 inches thick. Let's stay with the English measuring system as this is most commonly used when boards or waves are described. But for those more used to metric measurements – 1 foot = 30.48 cm and 1 inch = 25.4 mm – thus we can easily translate the board into metric. A hybrid sits somewhere in between a longboard and a shortboard. It is about 6.5 to 8 feet long, 21-22 inches wide and 2.5-3.5 inches thick.

Besides the dimensions, there are a few other things to take note of. The board should not be too heavy and, above all, it should have no sharp edges. Most injuries occur in surfing caused by your own board or by some other person's board. The most dangerous parts of the board are the tip of the nose and the fins. Thus the nose should be rounded and the fins should have no sharp edges (if necessary smooth off the edges with sandpaper or get a board with those newly developed rubber fins). For the beginner it does not matter whether the board has one, two or three fins. The rails of the board should similarly also be smoothly rounded.

A surfboard is made out of a polyurethane core with a fibreglass laminate on the outer surface. The glass is easily damaged so therefore a surfboard must always be handled carefully. The ceiling of the surfing shop is a favourite cause for the first ding when you lift a board up for inspection. So watch out! If, despite all the good advice and the greatest care, you have damaged the board somehow, you must get it repaired as quickly as possible. Otherwise the soft core mentioned earlier would soak up water, and after a while, the board will become heavier and it will be destroyed.

From left to right:
Shortboard, gun, hybrid,
Mini-Malibu, longboard
(Photo: Menges/Diel)

When buying a second-hand board you must check that the board does not show any cracks on the surface that have not been repaired, that the fins are firmly fixed and that the foam is not lifting at any place. If the board has brown discoloured spots, this means that at those spots water has already penetrated into the board.

A good alternative to purchasing is to rent a board on the spot. Many surfing shops have, amongst other things, boards especially for beginners to hire. Also most snowboarding or windsurfing shops can possibly be of help in the search for a board to hire. But remember: long, thick, wide and no sharp edges!

1.2.2 The Wetsuit

How long you can stay in the water will largely depend on your clothing – the wetsuit. It would be a pity, especially when the conditions are good, to start freezing after ten minutes in the water.

The wetsuit is made from a kind of rubber called neoprene. Unlike the so-called 'dry-suits' often used for windsurfing, which protect the whole body from the cold water, neoprene suits work on a different principle. Water becomes trapped between the suit and the body and is warmed by your own body temperature. The next time you go under, the warm water is flushed out and changes place with fresh cold water, which is then warmed up again. The wetsuit must fit snugly on the body so that not too much water can penetrate i.e., the body does not have to warm up too much water. The suit should also sit relatively tightly on the arms, round the neck and the legs. The thickness of the neoprene determines how much the coldness of the water and the wind can reach the body from the outside.

This brings us to another important feature of a wetsuit -- comfort. Too close a fit makes movement in the water difficult, and you are going to move a great deal. The same applies to thick suits that are on the one hand very warm, but on the other also very heavy. Many of the neoprene suits used by windsurfers or divers are therefore unsuitable for surfing. The thickness of the neoprene should be not more than 3 mm unless you are going to surf in extremely cold waters. The arms and legs of most surfing suits are 1 mm thinner than the rest. Very often you will find a number combination on the suit e.g., 3/2. This means 3 mm neoprene on the body part and 2 mm on the arms and legs.

Surfing suits come in various combinations, for example the 'full suit' or 'steamer' with long legs and sleeves, or the 'spring suit' with short sleeves and legs. To begin with use a suit with long legs. The sleeves can be either long or short. Long sleeves keep the warmth in but limit movement when paddling. If you choose a suit with long sleeves make sure that a piece of elastic material has been let into the shoulders – it makes paddling easier.

The final decision is dependent on the price, your personal warmth requirements, where you are going to use it and of course what you look like in it (remember Captain Kirk always looked cool).

You will often find that you get a rash on certain spots on the body from wearing the wetsuit. This is caused by the neoprene rubbing. To protect yourself you can get a special T-shirt made out of Lycra or a similar material – so-called wet-shirts or rash guards that are worn under the suit. Smearing Vaseline on the sensitive places offers another solution to prevent the rubbing. You can also wear the Lycra shirt without the suit to protect yourself against sunburn when surfing in warm water.

Just a few tips to extend the life of your wetsuit. Whenever possible, after each use, you should rinse your suit in fresh water. Besides this you should not leave your suit to dry in the sun. It is perfectly sufficient to hang it on a clothes hanger or over a washing line. The water will automatically run out and it will dry without the aid of the sun.

If you do not want to buy a wetsuit straight away, try checking out the surf shops where you can often find a suit for hire.

1.2.3 Wax and Leash

Wax

For a windsurfer it is the foot straps, for the snowboarder it is the binding and for the surfer it is the wax. Wax prevents the surfer from slipping off the wet board, which is logically wet when in the water. Each time, before you go into the water, the whole upper-side of the board must be completely waxed. The rear two-thirds of the board are important (this is where the feet stand) as well as the side edges of the forward two-thirds (this is where you hold the board when you duck through the waves). There is a special wax for each different water temperature. For the different degrees of colder water the wax must possess more consistency – 'stickiness' (soft wax for cold water and hard wax for warm water). The surface of the board should not be hot from the sun before you wax it. If this is the case simply hold the board in the water before you start waxing. You can do the same with a piece of wax that has sat in the sun and become soft.

If the board, at some stage, gathers a thick hardened surface after repeated waxing, it is sufficient to roughen up the surface with a so-called wax comb (you should buy one of these when you purchase your first piece of wax). By doing this the wax will grip again. If you run out of wax and you have left the wax comb in the car, the surface can also be roughened up using a handful of sand.

Many surfers use a so-called 'grip deck' glued on to the board. This is a development of the 'rubber daisies' that your mother used to put in the bottom of the bathtub so that the 'little darling' would not slip. The grip deck is glued on the board exactly where the surfer places his feet. This affords as good a grip as wax and saves the trouble of having to wax your board all the time. Nevertheless, for the beginner, waxing is still recommended because he will never stand on the same spot on the board all the time. It is hard to predetermine just exactly where the grip deck should be stuck on the board. We will return to this in the section later on 'Equipment for the Advanced'.

Leash

The 'leash' is an extremely practical and pleasant accessory. It resembles a lead made out of rubber. One end is attached to the end of the surfboard, and the other end is fixed to the surfer's ankle using a Velcro fastener. The leash saves a lot of trouble and effort if you fall off the board or you have to let go of it. You do not have to chase your board to the beach, swimming after it.

When buying the leash make sure it is equipped with a Velcro fastener with a simple opening mechanism. This is because if the leash gets caught up in something in the water, you must be able to open it with one movement (more about this in the section 'Equipment for the Advanced'). At the end where the leash joins the board there should be a so-called 'railsaver'. This is made from a piece of strong tear proof material, about 20 cm long, which prevents the leash from cutting into the polyester side of the board. At the end of the railsaver, the leash is attached to the board through the so-called 'plug' using a nylon rope. If you have to knot this piece of nylon you should use your very best mega-double sailor's knot. What good is the best leash if the knot slips and you are left there with your leash without a board attached to it?

But watch out! As much as it is nice not to continually keep losing your board, to have a 2 m solid hard object (your surfboard) strapped to your leg in the water is really quite dangerous. The leash is very elastic. If the board is washed away by a wave the leash can be stretched to its utmost limit. When the wave passes, the board springs back like a harpoon. This usually happens exactly at the moment when you have just surfaced to take a deep breath, and you are thinking "Uh hh! Where's my board?" Many of us have collected a few real "smashing" looking scars this way. In order to avoid this, you should always surface with your hands shielding your head. At the same time keep your eyes open and look around to find where your board is coming from in order to catch it. You should get into the habit of always automatically adopting the position of shielding your head when surfacing, because not only the board of a beginner has the habit of shooting back.

1.3   Preparation

*S*urfing is a very strenuous and physical sport. Therefore some preparation at home is important. Surfing can be made more fun by keeping physically fit. You can paddle longer without tiring and therefore you can surf longer. You can lose your fear of being held under by a wave if you have practised diving and holding your breath under water in the swimming pool beforehand. Some surfers maintain that you do not need any preparation as you can best learn surfing by simply surfing. Of course this is easy to say if you live five minutes away from the beach in Australia or California and can keep yourself fit by surfing regularly. But for those of us who live away from the ocean and perhaps can only spend a few weeks surfing, it is essential to carry out some preparation. Who wants to return to the beach after the first wave because your arms feel like jelly?

The main muscles that are used in surfing are the shoulder, back and upper arm muscles. The chest and neck muscles are also used a lot – in general the whole of the upper body is brought into play. The most tiring thing in surfing is not the actual surfing but the continuous paddling (for longer rides and lots of manoeuvres the leg muscles also play an important role). If you already own a board, you should practise paddling on your local lake. In this way, you can get a feeling for the correct position on home ground. A friend of ours ties his surfboard with the leash to the side of the swimming pool and practises paddling on the spot – this is also a way. For those who have not yet got a surfboard (or pool), or find it embarrassing to turn up at the local lake with a surfboard, we recommend regular swimming as the best preparation for surfing. The most useful stroke is the crawl. This uses practically the same muscles as the paddling movement. Besides this, swimming longer distances underwater is very helpful as well. Other then swimming, press-ups and similar exercises will be useful, preferably done in front of the television with a surfvideo playing.

Something that can be determined easily at home is your preferred way of standing on the surfboard. If you have been snow- or skateboarding before, you will know already whether you stand naturally with your left foot (regular foot) or with the right foot (goofy foot) forward. For those who do not yet know which way they would stand there are two simple ways of finding out. The first is jumping up from a press-up into a sideways standing position as if you were leaping onto the surfboard. Most of the time your subconscious will automatically find the correct position for you. The important thing is not to spend too long in the press-up position thinking about it – just simply jump up straight away.

The second way, concerns your so-called 'take-off leg'. This will always stand to the rear since, when surfing, this leg is the one that needs the most power. To find this out simply take a run and jump as if you were scoring a basket in basketball, or doing a long jump over a puddle. The take-off leg is the one with which you lead off when jumping. If, after all this, you are still not quite sure, you should simply rely on the result of your first attempt. Some time or other you will notice that when you stand up on the surfboard you are continually getting entangled in the leash. This is because, despite everything that your subconscious (and our smart advice) told you, your left foot is the one that belongs to the rear. This is the moment that you turn out to be a goofy after all.

2   The First Wave

ow you have the right surfboard, a suitable wetsuit, you have waxed your board, you have been swimming up and down, over and under water in the swimming pool, and now you are standing on the beach. You are ready to go. But isn't there something still missing? Well of course! - It is the right wave.

2.1   The Right Waves for the Beginner

If you listen to other surfers, you will often hear, "There are some unreal waves out there – perfect lines", and so on and so forth. You are immediately tempted to grab your surfboard and rush off into the water. But there are waves and waves and not everyone of them is surfable. What should the beginner be watching out for? Waves which look as if they have just come out of the latest surfing magazine often hide some danger. So do not just paddle out anywhere. Let's begin with the search for your first wave and make sure we know what to avoid.

To start with the waves should not be very high. This means that when you look at a surfer who is riding a wave, the wave should not be 'overhead' i.e., higher than the head of a surfer standing in an upright position. Although you should start your first few attempts mainly in white water or in the foam of a broken waves, large waves further out mostly give the indication of having a strong undercurrent. The beginner should also avoid these. He will also often have difficulty in being able to recognise strong currents. Because of this it is very wise to spend some time just watching and observing the sea and its movements. If there are surfers in the water note whether they are being pulled out to sea rapidly when they paddle out. Surfers, who are farther out, waiting for a wave may be paddling 'on the spot' in order to hold their position. This is a further indication that there is a strong current running.

In many countries, where there are lifeguards, there is a warning system. Flag signals are used to indicate sea dangers on any particular day. The beginner should learn the flag signals as follow (Please note that different colours may mean different things in some countries. You should therefore always check with the local lifeguards beforehand.):

Green Flag: Jump into your wetsuit and get out there (no danger!)

Yellow Flag: Not quite safe, but as long as you do not paddle out too far it is worth a try (watch out for currents and waves!).

Red Flag: Get out your camera and watch the hot rippers as they surf – beginners should not waste their time in the water (waves too high – strong currents running – danger!)

In addition to the information from the signal flags, there are also boundary flags that indicate the swimming zone. You should definitely keep clear of these zones. If you do venture into them you could find that the lifeguards will confiscate your surfboard.

Back to your first wave. If there are swimmers outside their marked off zones, you must keep particularly well clear of these also. It is preferable to go a few hundred metres farther away in the water. Make sure that wherever you want to practise there are not many swimmers, boogie-boarders or surfers around in the water. The beginner needs lots of space. It is quite obvious, however, that you should not go off into the wide wet far away from all the life-saving Baywatch models. Someone must be available to keep a watching eye on you.

Now to the wave itself. As a beginner you should look for the foam tips of the wave. The foam that appears on the top of the wave as it breaks should roll down continuously as the wave travels towards the beach. As it reaches the beach it should run out smoothly. Waves that pound the shoreline as they break on to the beach (called 'shore breaks') are dangerous. Watch out for damaged fins and breaking your surfboard!

Now a word about the sea bottom. The best waves for beginners break on to sandy beaches. This is not because of their quality. The reason is more that, in comparison to other bottom types, they will actually present less danger of you hurting yourself. Waves that break on to reefs, or above submerged reefs, are totally unsuitable for the beginner. Areas where there are rocks or other objects such as a harbour wall are also unsuitable – unfortunately some of the best waves are found in these areas. But do not lose heart!

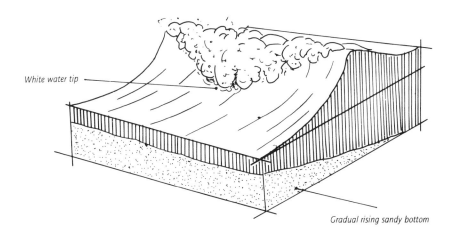

White water tip

Gradual rising sandy bottom

A continuous rolling wave breaking on a sandy bottom
(Drawing: Stefan "Muli" Müller)

2.2 Get Ready (on the Beach)

So you thought you could just simply jump in the water? Well, first of all here are a few dry exercises for doing on the beach. This will make surer that you turn yourself into a real clown on the beach from the word go – but so what? As a starter you should do some warming-up exercises in order to avoid sprains and cramps. Start with the muscles that you will be using later to paddle with i.e., the arm and shoulder muscles.

You can also try out on the beach how you should lie on the board in order to paddle. Lay your surfboard down on the sand and push the fins into the sand so that you can lie down without breaking them. You should lie on the board with your chest somewhere just forward of the middle of the board. You should lie with head, shoulders and chest raised to form a hollow in the back. The actual paddling movement is very similar to the arm movement when doing the crawl. Keep your fingers together and pull the arms to the rear alongside the surfboard. Make sure that you pull all the way through – from the tip of the board right through to the tail and out of the water (in this case lying on the beach -- out of the sand). Your legs should be kept together and your toes stretched out to the rear. The best thing to do is to keep your shins slightly raised out of the water so that the water resistance is lessened. This position is very strenuous for the beginner, and the back muscles will soon tire. After a few days of surfing, however, you will have built up the necessary muscles.

Now we turn to the movement of standing up. You should also practise this on the beach to start with. Lay down on the surfboard as already described above with your head up and your shoulders hollowed etc. Grab the rails with your handst at about the spot where your shoulders are in relation to the board. Your arms will be slightly angled in this posture. Now we come to actually standing up. Press up from the board and jump with both feet at once on to the surfboard. You must jump into a sideways stance with your feet apart. The forward foot should be a little in front of the middle of the board and your rear foot about 30 cm from the tail of the surfboard. To practise this do a press-up and then jump up into the standing position. Later, however, the action must become one flowing movement i.e., as you press up with your arms, the jump into the standing position is done almost simultaneously.

It is important that this movement becomes automatic so that when you are in the water you do not have to think about it at all – nothing like 'Err, well – what was it? Hold on to the leash, press-up or what?" Keep on practising jumping into the standing position until it becomes a natural thing to do. Far better to look a bit of a clown now, but coolly surf down the waves later! Now we can start walking in the direction of the water. I bet you thought you would never get there!

2.3   How Do I Get out?

When we say "Get out" or "Out" in further sections of this book we mean "Get out on the sea!" The opposite is "In!" which means getting back to the beach and into the arms of your girl- or boyfriend.

For your first day of surfing you have hopefully selected a sandy beach with little or no shore break, and where the white water of the waves breaking further out, rolls more or less gently right up on to the beach. This is important because the white water creates a natural barrier for you. If your technique is not good enough to push through this white water, you will never reach the somewhat dangerous area where the large waves are breaking. It is another story with waves that break on a reef bottom. One can often paddle around the white water and get out amongst large breaking waves without even getting your hair wet. But when you are there all of a sudden out between the other surfers and amongst some sizeable waves you sit there wondering what the hell you are supposed to do now.

The big question now is, "How do I get out as far as is necessary?"

2.3.1   Entering the Water

After a thorough warm-up session, put your leash on – goofys on the left leg and regulars on the right. Now pick up your surfboard under the arm. The best way is to place it under the arm on the side where you wear your leash. The leash will dangle between the end of the board and your foot. It is too easy to get caught up in your leash as you walk to the water and make a complete fool of yourself as you fall over the board. To avoid this, grab the leash roughly about the middle of its length with the same hand that you are holding the board. Doing this effectively halves the length of the leash, and it does not tumble about any more. Now choose a spot where you can wade out as far as possible to meet the white water foam coming in. Keep your surfboard still under your arm as you enter the water. Do not drag it along in the water. You must keep control of your surfboard at all times, otherwise the next wave will smash it against your shin or some other part of your body. Now we are slowly getting closer – do not panic when the first white water comes rushing in. At all costs do not hold the board in front of you as a shield. You are likely to find it smashed into your face with the next wave. The board must remain horizontal, held next to your body with the fins pointing downwards. Once you are far enough out in the water and you have got through the first few waves, you can lie down on the surfboard and begin to paddle.

2.3.2   Paddling

Paddling is what you will actually be doing for most of the time when you go surfing. You will be paddling out to sea, paddling to get over a wave, paddling to catch a wave and paddling back to the beach etc. Sooner or later it is going to be as natural as running.

When you start your first attempt, make sure that the surfboard is lying flat on the surface of the water. The nose of the board must peep out of the water a little. Not too much otherwise you will be pushing water in front of you rather than gliding over it. This will mean that you will not be able to reach the right speed when paddling for a wave. do not forget what we practised on the beach: chest roughly about the middle, head up, overstretched back, toes stretched out, shins just out of the water and pull through well with the arms. It all sounds simple, and it is, but one should not underestimate paddling. Paddling is one of the most important things in surfing. Some would of course say, "Well yes, but what about standing up, balancing on the surfboard and riding the wave?"

Wrong paddling position – back overstretched, position is too far back on the board and legs are spread in the water. (Photo: Menges/Diel)

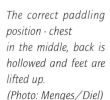

The correct paddling position - chest in the middle, back is hollowed and feet are lifted up. (Photo: Menges/Diel)

Well, of course this is all important, but if you do not build up enough speed when paddling because you are not lying on the board properly, or you are using the wrong paddling technique, you will not even reach let alone catch a wave. Perfecting the paddling movement and building up the necessary muscles are therefore very important for the beginner. If you want to be a good surfer, you must be in a position to be able to paddle fast and effectively. When you are sitting on your board in two or three years time (sorry, only a joke) and a wave is approaching, you must be lying on the right spot on the board and with a few paddling strokes be able to match the speed of the wave. If not, the wave will simply pass by underneath. More on this later.

After you have slipped off your board a couple of times and you seem always to be thrashing about on the same spot, slowly, you will start moving forwards.

2.3.3   Dealing with Broken Waves

As a beginner, of course, you do not want to go right out to sea where the big waves are breaking. You will much rather try surfing the white water further inside during your first attempts. But despite this, sometime or other, you will have to venture further out and over the first wave. When looking at the waves you will often ask yourself how it is at all possible to get through them. However, using the right technique – 'duck-diving' – which we will describe later – and the correct amount of endurance and practice, it will not be a problem any more for you. Duck-diving is quite a complicated technique and it can take a long time before you can master it. This is why you should, initially, use the beginner's technique to get over the first few lines of white water. According to how far you have managed to walk out, and how deep the water is where you are, there are several methods. If you are still able to stand in the water and a wave is rolling towards you, simply push yourself off the ground and lay the board in front of you and on to the foam, pushing and supporting yourself on the board as far as possible. Make sure you get a good grip on your board beforehand. If you are further out to sea, and you are already lying on the board and paddling, there are also several ways of pushing through waves. Firstly you can get off the board and simply dive through the wave without the board. The board is pulled along behind you by not holding on to the leash but, so not to have your fingers squashed, by grabbing the railsaver (you know that piece of nylon which connects the leash to the board). Another way is to do a kind of press-up on the board. This is done by paddling with speed towards the white water. Just before you meet the wave, you press up your body from the board – like in a press-up – so that the water can pass between your body and the board. This method, however, will only work in small waves.

Duck-diving through a wave
(Photo: Tony King, Surf Travel Co.)

If you meet a larger wave, in the split second as it breaks just in front of you or over you, you have probably already forgotten everything that we have explained. You wish you were far away, now! In such a case we recommend the emergency exit, or as we say bail out. Let go of your board and dive down as deep as you can. Probably not the best of solutions, but it is often the only way to make a quick getaway. It is important that you make sure that no other surfer is behind you before you let go of the board and dive. The wave would have slammed your board into the other surfer's face.

This variant is, therefore, really only for an emergency. For surfers, letting go of the board is a foul. Other surfers can easily get injured this way. Another disadvantage is that it often takes longer to gain control of the board after you come up because, first of all, you have to pull the board back towards you, by which time the next wave has arrived.

By the way, please remember always to surface with your hands protecting your head. Sometimes the board is immediately above you when you surface. If you do not have the protection of your arms and hands, your board and your head will get dented.

Another tip - when surfacing after bailing out you will want to pull your board back quickly but it often sticks in the water like a buoy or anchor. No panic - just swim a stroke or two towards the board. This releases the pressure caused by the water pushing over it and allows you to quickly regain control.

2.4   How Do I 'Catch' a Wave?

You are now where you wanted to be in the beginning - on the ocean to surf. This means that, up until now, everything was just preparation, but now we can really get down to business. Let's catch a wave and go surfing! Lying, kneeling or stand ... oh well, OK, more of this later. But it does not matter which way you ride a wave. To surf, first of all you have to catch the wave and the wave has to take you with it. It all looks so simple, but it is not that easy. It is all a question of good timing and the right judgement of the advancing wave or white water.

First of all – a quick look at the sequence of actions:

You are sitting or lying on the board looking out to sea. A wave that looks as if you could surf it approaches. Paddling, you turn the board to point towards the beach. You glance over your shoulder to get a better look at the advancing wave, and at the same time you start paddling strongly towards the beach. The wave picks you up from behind and now you mobilise all your strength to increase your paddling speed. The wave pushes you and all of a sudden you are gliding towards the beach without you having to do anything. You are surfing.

Now that was simple, wasn't it? Nevertheless the part which gives most beginners the greatest problem is paddling to catch the wave. Even more so later on when they have to stand up just at the moment they are being picked up by the wave.

2.4.1 Paddling for a Wave

Just imagine that you want to jump on to a moving train. You would hardly think of standing by the rails and, at the right moment – here we go – just jump on the train. It is more likely that you would run alongside the train, for a short time reach the same speed as the train, and then, at the right moment, jump on. The more you can match the speed of the train, the easier it will be for you to jump, on and hold on firmly.

Well, of course the example is a little far-fetched but it does serve to emphasise the key point about paddling for a wave.

The aim is to match, for a short moment, the speed of the wave by paddling.

It is only then that the wave will pick you up and take you along, and will not simply pass by under you.

What exactly is the key?

First of all let's return to the beginning of the situation we described where you were lying or sitting on your surfboard, gazing out to sea. The beginner is recommended to start off using the foam of a wave that has already broken. But do not be mistaken, this foam has often enough power to either rip you off the board or shoot you off towards the beach at breathtaking speed. A white water wave is approaching. You decide you are going to have a go at this one. You turn your board with a few paddling movements so that it is pointing towards the beach, and you begin to paddle forwards. The main point here is to do this early enough. Of course if you watch the pros it will appear that they do all of this in the very last second. That is, when the wave is directly behind them they make a couple of paddling strokes, and hey presto, there they are standing on the board. You are not quite there yet. The beginner must begin to paddle as early as possible. This gives you more time to build up your speed. You paddle with all you have got, glancing over your shoulder occasionally in order to judge how far away the wave still is. Now comes the critical moment. The wave is directly behind you and lifts the board up. Now you have to put everything into it, and we mean everything. Paddle as fast as you can. It is as if all those hours spent in the swimming pool were the training for this moment.

Now this is when most beginners make the mistake of stopping paddling too early, namely as soon as they feel the board being lifted up behind them. The lifting of the board must not be the signal to stop, rather the starting gun to paddle like mad. This is important. Even if you think you can feel that the wave is beginning to take you, because everything starts to move a little faster, you still have to give two or three powerful strokes with your arms. And now – yes, now – the wave is taking you with it, and the fun starts.

Let's look at it once again:
- Start paddling towards the beach early and build up your speed.
- At the moment the wave picks you up from behind, mobilise all your strength and paddle like mad.
- When you think you have caught the wave, make two to three additional powerful strokes.

Especially for the last point it is important that you have the right position on the board. If you are lying too far forwards, just when the board is picked up from behind, the tip of the board will dig into the water usually resulting in a small somersault.

If you are lying too far towards the rear, it has the effect as if you have thrown an anchor overboard. The wave will then be too fast for you. It will run underneath or over the top of you. Generally speaking, you should tend to lie just a little to the front. It can well happen that you will do a nose-dive (the tip digs deep into the water), but the wave will rather more tend to take you with it than if you had been lying too far to the rear. You will learn to control the nose-dive after it has happened two or three times.

The start point for a successful ride is the right balance on the board. Take a little time practising in calm water, exploring the ins and outs of the correct position. Earlier on we said that the beginner should start using the white water of a broken wave. If you feel confident enough there is no reason why you should not try it out with an unbroken wave. Our experience is that this will usually end up in a few funny wipe-outs, but that the beginner will develop a feeling for the waves quicker, and it is simply a lot more fun. So if you feel sure, and have been finding the foam a little bit boring, give it a try and paddle out to a real wave. However there are one or two things that you should watch out for, and which are different than when you were starting with the foam.

The size of the waves should be so that you do not get a funny feeling just looking at them. Also, even for the most daring, the height of the wave should not be more than a metre.

Take care – when you are standing on the beach everything looks different than when you are lying on your stomach paddling towards a wave. All of a sudden, the waves look enormous. Lay down in front of a small child and look up (OK – just imagining this should do the trick). Even a one-metre high dwarf will look like a giant. It is the same with the waves – so take good care.

Just like when you were paddling for the white water, you are lying on your board and now an unbroken wave is coming towards you. It still has its full height, and is not yet pushing any white water.

Now comes the difficult part. When you start paddling towards the beach, the wave has got to be just before it breaks. It will already be very steep without breaking. This means that you have to judge, absolutely correctly, the speed of the incoming wave, and, at first, this is not at all easy to do. With a bit of luck, and having again done a few starts in the white water (because the wave broke too early), you will soon have this wired. If the wave breaks before it reaches you, use the foam to surf on, and paddle out a little further the next time - "Hey, I said just a little", said the surfing instructor just before his pupil disappeared over the horizon. If the wave runs through and under you and breaks a few metres past you, then you must wait for the wave a few metres nearer to the beach. After a few attempts you will soon find just the right spot.

Naturally you can orient yourself on the other surfers around. However, we have already mentioned that the beginner should keep away from other surfers; somewhere under supervision, but generally speaking on his own to try out the first starts.

This is important! If you find that a surfer is already on the wave that is approaching, do not start paddling at all. Wait for the next wave. A surfer who is standing has absolute right of way. Try to get out of the surfer's way. If you do not know which way is "out of the way", simply stay where you are and do not move about. Better surfers should then be able to avoid you. We will return later to discuss the exact right of way rules.

Back to paddling! Let us assume that you are at the right place, at the right time, and you have begun to paddle towards the beach also at just the right moment. The wave is about to break, and it is directly behind you. The feeling of being picked up from behind by the wave is naturally much more intense than when starting in foam. After all, a metre high wave will lift you up a metre. Otherwise the sequence remains the same. The wave lifts you up, and you put everything into paddling. This is your first wave – go for it! The wave pushes you forward and the speed picks up. Now for the famous last two powerful paddling strokes with the arms, and – whoops, the nose of the board digs into the water and you do the usual forward loop.

Never mind – just try again. Clearly, because the wave face is relatively steep, there is somewhat of an edge at the bottom.

As soon as you have made your two last paddling strokes, take a firm hold of the sides of the board and move your weight a little towards the rear. Again, here you will have to try it several times in order to discover the right feeling.

The most important thing, however, is that you actually achieve being picked up by a wave. Calling on our example at the beginning once again:

– **You've jumped on to the moving train, but now you have got to hold on to enjoy the ride.**

2.4.2 Catching a Wave

In this part of the book we are going to try to teach you something, that, being quite honest, can only really be learned by trying it out yourself. You may read this book over and over again but surfing can only be learnt by surfing, and not by doing some or other form of drill, or by reading clever books like this one. It is simply a question of going through the written descriptions and picking up a tip or two from us, so that the learning process is made a little easier and quicker. If only you fall off your board a little less often because of our tips, we will be smiling from ear to ear.

Surfing, in its broadest sense of gliding on a wave, can be done in several different ways. Simply lying down, kneeling, of course standing up, and even completely without a board. The important ways are for the beginner lying down and generally of course the 'proper' way of surfing – standing up. The latter calls for a degree of balance, timing, and above all practice. We will not go into surfing in the kneeling position, although there are a number of surfers, – so called kneeboarders – who have made this a speciality, and who can do some very radical things in radical waves. Other than that, you only surf on your knees if you have not been able to make it to the standing position. This is then more or less rather by chance and in order to avoid a wipe-out. In short we want you to become a 'real surfer', who, standing up on his board, can master the waves of this world. But now a few words about your first attempts at surfing lying down – just like the old saying "you have to be able to walk before you can run".

2.4.2.1 The Prone Position

As a result of your paddling efforts, a wave has actually picked you up – but, what now? Quite simple – just enjoy the ride! Hold on to the sides of the board, and simply let it run, or as they say, 'Go with the flow'.

You will notice at some point that you appear to be too heavy for the wave. The farther the wave travels away from the point where it broke, the less power it has. You are left behind, so to speak, and the wave runs through underneath you. If you are getting too close to the beach, just roll off the board so that, logically, you stop immediately. After your next successful attempt at catching a wave, try out a few things like the following. You can steer very simply by changing your centre of mass on the board. Because you will have both hands holding the sides of the board, you only need to lift it with your right (or left) hand and you will turn to the left (or right). Try surfing in a line across the foam. Now steer left or right so that you surf almost parallel to and along the line of the foam. This all serves to give you a feeling for the waves. How fast is the wave, and how should I change my balance so that I can glide along as far as possible? When all this gets a little boring, then it is time to ascend into the league of 'stand up surfers'.

2.4.2.2 Standing up

Surfing in the stand up position is actually what this book is all about. Even when the moment that you are standing and gliding on a wave lasts only a few seconds, the joy you experience will capture you. You will want more - and you will get more. The more you practice, the longer you will be able to ride on the wave - and these rides will, step by step, get even larger. But, first of all - back to the beginning.

Now that you know how to paddle for a wave, and how to surf lying down, the next step is just a little one. But, as Armstrong said when he visited the moon "One small step for man, but a large step on the way to becoming a surfer" or something like that.

OK! Let's get going: paddle, push down the accelerator and two final strokes ...? Do you still remember all the dry land exercises, embarrassing as they were? The jumps-up into the stand from the push-up position? Never mind whether you are a goofy or a regular – i.e., with the right foot or the left forward. That is exactly what you have to do now. It really will be an advantage if you did the exercises on the beach earlier once or twice too often. The key is automation. Back to the wave! Above all, it is important that you only try to stand up when the wave has really and truly picked you up. Generally, most beginners tend to try to stand up straight away, at the moment when the wave has picked them up and pushes them from behind. Because of this we have always taken the trouble to emphasise that when you think the wave has picked you up, you must make two further strokes. Otherwise the wave will run away underneath you just as you try to stand up.

Pushing up into the standing position
(Photo: Menges/Diel)

Small, gentle waves are not only fun for the beginner.
(Photo: Uli from Wave Tours)

This often has certain similarity with a sinking Titanic. When using the relatively small surfboards you cannot simply stand without the necessary momentum. So, only stand up when you really have got the wave. Of course, you will fall off the board the first few times you try it, despite having done all the dry land exercises often enough. This is all part of it. If you have equipped yourself from the beginning with a long broad surfboard, then it will make everything much easier. It is easier to maintain your balance, and you will succeed quicker. On your next surfing holiday the board can already get a few centimetres shorter but for now the large board is just right. There is always the possibility that you can adopt a kneeling position before you stand up. You will probably do this for the first few attempts anyway. However, this way of learning is not recommended. One quickly gets too used to kneeling before standing. This leads not only to cuts and bruises of the knee and a damaged wetsuit, but also later on, just at the moment when you want to stand up, you will waste a lot of precious time. This is why it is best to go directly from lying down to standing up. Your stance should be as wide as possible; this means that your front foot and your back foot should be placed relatively far apart from each other – but please, do not do the splits! If you have done snowboarding or skateboarding you will already know the best way to stand safely on the board. One will have a somewhat broader stance, the other a slightly narrower stance. Your back foot should be about 30 cm from the end of the board, with your front foot placed just a bit in front of the middle. In the end of course everyone stands slightly differently. The grip deck gives a good indication where your feet should be. You just have to try it out. You will soon find your individual preference. If you stand too far back, you will brake the board too hard. The wave will run through underneath you because you will have lost momentum. If you stand too far forward the nose will dig into the water and whoops ... well, you already know this.

For the first attempts you should also bend and flex your knees as deeply as possible. This means you should not stand upright straight away. The centre of mass of your body is thus lower and you can maintain your balance better and avoid falling off the board.

And now the most important tip: practice, practice, practice, again and again and again. Above all never give up!

There will come a moment when you are suddenly standing and you have no idea how you did it. We can still recall a friend of ours, whose nickname funnily enough was "Fish". All week Fish kept on falling off the board, had swallowed a lot of water, and constantly swore about this "absolutely stupid" sport. We had just ridden a wave and were paddling back out as Fish, standing up, came surfing towards us on a screamer of a wave. We will never forget the look on his face. He will not forget probably our completely puzzled looks either.

2.5 How Do I Get back to the Beach?

We assume that you have followed our advice and have chosen a sandy beach for your first attempts. This means that where you have entered the water you can easily come out again on to dry land. This is not always the case with reef ledges and points. You have just decided to call it a day with your surfing session – for whatever reason – you are hungry, tired or cold. It is important that you never overload yourself completely. You must always have some reserves left. Sometimes you may find a few obstacles on your way to the beach. So let's start with a safety tip:

If you ever find yourself really in difficulty, signal the SOS by waving at people on the beach or at other surfers, where possible, with both hands above your head.

Let's hope that you will never have to do this. The simplest way to get back to the beach is to ride a wave in the prone position, or to let yourself be washed on to the beach by the white water of a broken wave. Here again do not forget to paddle to catch it. Try, as far as possible, to keep in the foam moving towards the beach. If you begin to lose momentum you can always do a couple of paddling strokes. This will keep you on the wave even when it is really too weak to take you with it.

On the way home you could meet the following problems:
1. Strong currents close to the beach, and
2. the shore break.

The first one is not a real problem. If the foam is unable to carry you with it, you can paddle with your own strength to the beach. If there is a current running parallel to the beach, caused by the sandbanks where the waves break, it will be a little more difficult. The water breaks on to the sandbanks and runs away in a kind of basin. At high tide sometimes these can be really deep. No waves break in this area, so you cannot use them to ride back to the beach. The water flows out of these basins sideways and creates currents. A tip! Never paddle for a long time against the current. Close to the beach you will be carried along several metres. do not panic – simply go with the current and constantly paddle in the direction of the beach. Sometime or other the current will let you go and you will succeed. But wait a minute, there is still a little obstacle – the shore break.

The shore break is the last obstacle. It hides a certain danger. You cannot surf this wave on the belly because it breaks directly on to the beach. If you are still lying on your board when it breaks, it means certain damage to the fins. So be careful – many a board has been broken into two or more pieces by the shore break. The trick here is to paddle up as far as you can to the edge of the last break, then get off the board and hold yourself on it. Lay one arm over it to stabilise it, and swim using leg strokes only (like the breast stroke kick) to the beach. Wait for a smaller wave and let yourself be pushed on to the beach. The advantage is that you will be standing in shallow water, and you already have your board under your arm and thus you can run out of the shore break zone. Dependant on how strong the shore break is it may actually be advisable to even race out of the water. The treacherous thing about the shore break is that the broken waves run back into the sea and create a kind of reverse current which tends to pull you back into the impact zone of the shore break. If you get stuck in there you will get a regular pounding on the head. So, get off the board in advance and swim, and finally run away from the wave – so to speak.

If you have managed this last hurdle you can take a deep breath. Now, your first surfing session was not all that bad, was it? If you listen very carefully you will surely hear somewhere in the background the group Pearl Jam singing, "Oh, I'm still alive".

3   Now Let's Surf!

*Y*our first attempts at surfing will have been restricted to paddling for a wave and just riding down it. Arriving at the bottom of the wave face you will probably only surf for a few metres and then slow down and fall off. The reason for this is that your momentum after the take-off will be very high. You will move faster than the wave and will so to speak overtake it. When your momentum and speed drop the wave will catch up with you as it breaks, and usually you will be knocked off the board. For the first few take-off and attempts at standing this is OK of course, but soon you should try to avoid only going straight. Try to surf to the left or right across the wave face shortly after you have caught it. This means you will no longer be surfing towards the beach but now parallel to it down the line of the breaking wave. You stay in front of the white water in the unbroken part of the wave.

The advanced surfer will build up speed by alternately swinging up and down the wave face. This looks really like riding the surf – he is a surf rider.

3.1   Riding a Wave

*T*o ride down the line of the wave it is important that the wave does not break along its whole length at the same moment. The wave breaks to the left or right. Along the length of the wave there is always a part that has not yet broken. The surfer will always try to surf a wave in his mind and think of trying to keep in front of the waves' white water and foam. Sometimes the waves break too early and quickly so that the surfer would not have time to get in front of the breaking wave, and he would be caught by the white water. The wave is "closing out" or the surfspot is not working. The surfer will probably decide to try another spot. If the wave slowly peels in one direction or the other you should give it a go.

Now, let's surf!
(Photo: Jeff Hornbaker, Quiksilver)

Viewing from the water in the direction of the beach when the wave breaks to the left we speak of a "left-hander" or a "left". If it breaks to the right then It is called a "right-hander" or a "right". This sounds logical enough, but it is often misunderstood. Remember – the direction of the breaking wave is described always from a viewpoint in the water looking in to the beach.

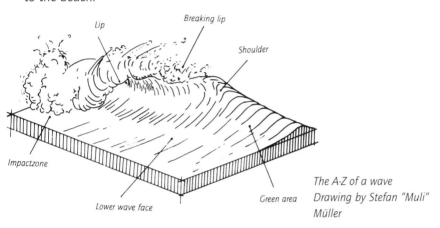

The A-Z of a wave
Drawing by Stefan "Muli" Müller

A goofy – someone who stands with the left foot to the rear – is surfing a left facing the wave. He is therefore surfing "frontside" on his "forehand" as we say. The regular, conversely, will have his face to the wave if it is a right. If you surf with your back to the wave you are surfing "backside" on your "backhand". The difference is that most surfers find it easier to surf frontside along a wave. The sequence of movements is more natural. The wave is always in sight, allowing you to react quicker when the wave changes. Some of the left breaking waves in the world were surfed for some time by goofys before they were mastered one day by a regular on his backhand. Meanwhile surfers and their equipment have reached such a high level, that surfing frontside or backside does only make a difference in particularly extreme wave conditions. Your first surfing experience, however, to keep it simple, should be done frontside on your forehand.

But how do you manage to surf along a wave at all? There are two basic techniques. One is to paddle for a wave in an angle to the straight ahead direction. The other way is to make a turn at the bottom of the wave up into the unbroken part of the wave. This latter technique is one of the most important manoeuvres for the advanced surfer – this is called the 'bottom turn'. For a good bottom turn, the efficient transformation of the speed, reached in surfing down the wave face into a good speed to surf along the wave face, is generally the starting point of a good ride. But more about this later. To begin with you should try to paddle for a wave in an angle. This means that instead of paddling straight towards the beach, you paddle diagonally down the line of the breaking wave – dependent on the wave, left or right. Using a clock as a guide, with the beach at 12 o'clock, paddle left towards 10 o'clock, or to the right to 2 o'clock. If you have paddled fast enough and not forgotten the last two arm strokes, you will be moving almost parallel to the beach. You should try this out for the first few times in the prone position, so that you can get the feeling you actually are going along the wave without losing speed.

Paddling for a wave in an angle is usually not the problem here. For the beginner it is more likely to be very difficult to recognise in which direction and where the wave is breaking. There is only one way out. Practice trying it out, and watching other surfers. Try guessing which direction a surfer will take as you watch him. So-called 'line-ups' are not only used by competent surfers to orientate themselves, but can also help the beginners. In general, the area where surfers sit in the water waiting for a wave is called the 'line-up'. This is the first orientation point used to predict where the waves will break. Quite logical isn't it? Why else would the surfers be sitting there?

Line-ups can also mean landmarks on the beach, which can be used as an aid when in the water to orientate yourself. A coloured beach umbrella, a particular tree or some scrub on a hill or dune can all be used to line yourself up with once you are in the water. If you find some good orientation points while you are still on the beach, later on when in the water you will find it easier to say which way the wave will break – to the right or to the left. A line-up helps also to recognise whether the current is carrying you too far. To summarise – orientation points on the beach can help you when in the water to know what is going on around you.

The aim is to surf in the unbroken part of the wave just in front of the white water.
(Photo: Menges/Diel)

3.2   The First Manoeuvres

In order to be able to surf successfully along a wave, from beginning to end, the next step is to learn the manoeuvres that will help you to hold your speed so that you are always surfing in front of the white water. Let's carry on where we left off: You paddle for a wave in an angled direction and you are up and riding in front of the white water. The wave is changing shape all the time. Sometimes the wall in front of you gets steeper and you speed up. It then becomes flatter again and you slow down. The degree of the slope of the wave face depends on the depth of the water. Shallow water creates steep waves. Sounds simple. But, what happens when after a slow section it turns into a quicker section? If you have not built up enough speed the faster section will break before you reach it, or it will break over you, and your ride will be over.

There are different techniques of building up or dropping off speed. The latter is of particular interest when a slower section follows a fast one, and you are zipping away in front of it because of the speed you have built up already. But, first of all the most important point – building up speed. In advanced surfing trimming your board is called 'pushing' or 'pumping' the board. You gain speed by alternately riding up and down the wave face. The initial speed of course comes from the take-off.

Basically, by changing your centre of mass onto the back foot you will slow down, and onto the front foot, you will speed up. Let's assume that you are a regular-foot, riding a wave to the right i.e., facing the wave (frontside). For a goofy-foot, the following will of course be the opposite. You are surfing diagonally along a wave (regular-foot frontside). Normally your position on the wave face is approximately halfway between the trough of the wave and its upper lip. You now lean a little towards the direction you want to go. The more you switch your balance, the more extreme your turn or curve will be. But hold it ... gently does it! You lean slightly towards the base of the wave face i.e., to the left. You give a little pressure downward on to the forward foot, and thus begin surfing down the wave. At the bottom of the wave you have gained enough speed, and with a change of balance now towards the wave face i.e., to the right, you swing up the wave face again. You surf upwards until you begin to lose speed and start to slow down. Now you surf down the wave again and so on.

If you have a good long running wave you can repeat this often, achieving a sort of rhythm. This is good, because all the uphill and downhill movements (this is starting to sound like a snowboard book) should be done with no sharp turns, rather more a fluid movement. Once you have successfully managed your first few rides you can try to unweight alternately in order to gain yet more speed. On top of the wave flex your knees. Just at the moment you begin to surf down, gently press down with the legs. At the foot of the wave face the centrifugal force will have almost automatically made you flex your knees again. If you now change your centre of mass towards the top of the wave, and unweight the board at the same time, you will gain momentum as you move up the wave face. Back at the top the wave will press your knees down together like a shock absorber. Now press down with the legs again and surf down the wave face. You will soon get the feeling for how the unweighting process works, because it is determined by the wave itself. The whole process is almost like when you try to get a child's swing in motion on your own. You can also imagine that you are on a snowboard or skis applying the classic up and down movement to go through turns. Above all it is important that during each movement you keep your eyes on the point where your turn will lead or where you want to end up after your turn.

To end your ride, or if the wave closes out in front of you and you have to abort your ride, there are two ways of doing this. One is called the 'kick-out' or 'flick off', and is done by turning the board up the wave, over the top and over the back of it. Watch out here – doing this can catapult you into the air. Nice to watch for the spectator, but dangerous for the surfer not only because the board is connected to the leash and the foot. You may land on your own board (thereby breaking it) or on another surfer. To avoid flying into the air, simply push down with the front foot as you arrive at the top of the wave, allowing you to actually ride over the back of the wave. Really cool, especially when you are able to lie down on your board just after you pushed over the wave and immediately begin to paddle out again after a good ride. The other way to exit a wave is to make a turn towards the beach and leave the closed out section behind you. When the white water catches you either lie down on the board, hold on tightly and surf towards the beach on your belly, or jump off the back of the board, pushing it towards the beach as you do. Generally the white water will wash over you and you will not get washed too far into the shore. You can now paddle quickly out to the line-up again.

The Bottom Turn

The 'bottom turn' is really only a turn at the bottom of the wave face. It is as important for the surfer as is the serve for a tennis player – for some the highlight of their talent, or for others 'just' the beginning for everything that follows. During the movements we have just described for the up and down on the wave face, you were already doing a small bottom turn. A real bottom turn, however, means that at the foot of the wave you not only lean towards the wave a little, but you also apply so much pressure on the inside rail that the board actually goes through the turn on its edge. The result is that you do not lose any momentum and you can continue surfing with full speed. This movement is very similar to carving when snowboarding. If you are leaning over far enough in the turn your hand will often touch the water (– the rear hand in case of a forehand bottom turn). When you surf down a wave and, at the bottom, lead with your rear hand pointing it in the direction of the water, you will automatically lay into the bottom turn a little more. During the turn pressure and weight is always on the rail closest to the wave face – the inside-rail of the board. When you unweight and take the pressure of the rail, the turn is completed and you surf up the wave face again setting up the next move.

Peter doing a forehand bottom turn. Weight is on the inside rail. (Photo: Menges/Diel)

The Top Turn

By doing a good bottom turn you will have speed left to be able to surf up the wave face again. More than likely you will even have too much, so that you could shoot up over the wave without a manoeuvre that allows you to slow down a little and change direction. Therefore at the top of the wave you will have to do a turn to surf back down it again.

This is done by applying strong pressure on the rear foot. You give your rear leg an additional push to press the tail of the board through the turn as if you were trying to push the water away with it. You simply push the tail through the turn. Your front foot is practically the pivot, and the rear one steers through the move.

Top turn - change of direction at the top of the wave
(Photo by Chiemsee, photographer: Xandi Kreuzeder)

The Cutback

A further manoeuvre to reduce speed, so not to race away from the wave, is the 'cutback'. In its simplest form it is merely a turn in the opposite direction to the breaking direction of the wave. You will need the cutback if you are too far out on the shoulder of the wave i.e., you are too far away from the breaking curl of the wave. This can often be the case when a mellower, slower part follows a steep, fast part of the wave. The sequence in detail:

You are surfing along a wave, and notice that you have too much speed as you are riding too far out on the shoulder. You are not able to use this speed because in front of you the wave is starting to get relatively flat. Time for a cutback. You make a turn in the direction of the bottom of the wave face by changing your balance on to the rear foot. The difference to the previously described top turn is that you continue turning by keeping

Cutback – a turn against the breaking direction of the wave.
(Photo by Chiemsee, photographer: Erik Aeder)

the pressure on the rear foot and thereby on the tail of the board until the nose of the board is pointing in the opposite direction to the breaking direction of the wave. This means you are really riding back to the more powerful part of the wave. Cutback!

Now the white water is coming towards you. You either do another turn in the 'correct' direction before the approaching foam reaches you, or you use the power of this foam to drive you in the original direction again. If you make a turn directly on to or with the foam (turning down the wave face), this will automatically drive you in the right direction. This latter move is called a 'rebound'. Of course, this is not an easy manoeuvre, but the rolling foam conveniently offers itself as a springboard to go back in the right direction. Done perfectly this is a very spectacular move. The rebound, done in conjunction with the cutback, mentioned earlier, is called a 'round house cutback'. We will look at this a little closer in the chapter for the advanced.

Surfing Backhand

Actually this is not a manoeuvre in itself. Despite this it is something that has to be constantly practised in order to master it. You are right, it feels a bit strange, but the more you practise it the more surfing backhand becomes natural. There are two main difficulties. First of all you are surfing with your back to the wave. You can hardly see what is happening behind you. In addition, to see what is happening to the wave behind you at all, you have to look constantly over your shoulder. Having to keep turning your head makes it more difficult to keep your balance. Also weighting and unweighting your board seems not to be so easy. Only practise will help. Here are a few tips before you try the manoeuvres we covered earlier on the backhand.

During a bottom turn you should make sure that your forward hand (goofy – left; regular – right) is stretched out, pointing towards the wave face. The forward hand towards the wave face? How? What do you mean?

Just imagine that you have to support yourself on your forward hand as you lean into the turn. This would of course be not in front of the body but behind it. This stance helps you to balance your body and to transfer your speed in the right direction. During the bottom turn your weight is on your heels, and at the moment you turn, your knees are fully bent. You are looking over your shoulder and focus on the point where your turn will take you. Your forward foot should be in an angle to the nose of the board – regulars around 2 o'clock and goofys around 10 o'clock (– the nose is at 12 o'clock).

The top turn comes a little easier if you shift your centre of mass relatively hard towards the bottom of the wave face. To start with you can simply try to push your bottom outwards as you turn. At the same time you push your rear foot towards the top of the wave. This gives the board a turning momentum.

Backside top turn
(Photo: O'Neill, photographer: Bill Morris)

To do a cutback you really only have to do a forehand turn in the opposite direction. With your face looking towards the bottom of the wave you make a turn against the breaking direction. The weighting is the same as the forehand bottom turn. Weight is on the toes, with the rear hand stretched in the direction of the water (– in front of the body), and your body leaning into the turn. Try to imagine that you are actually doing a forehand turn. This way the manoeuvre will almost seem like the easiest backside manoeuvre of all.

To practise surfing on your backhand, a 'point break' is the best spot because the wave only breaks in one direction. You are automatically forced to surf backhand (– for goofys a right wave, and for regulars a left one). If there are only beach breaks, use one of your sessions to practise only backhand. Stick to it, and do not fall back into surfing on your forehand until it works.

3.3 General Tips for the Beginner

- At the beginning keep away from other water sportsmen.
- Never surf alone or without supervision.
- Observe the waves rather one time too many before you enter the water.
- Give it everything when paddling for a wave plus two extra strokes – even when you believe that you have actually caught the wave.
- If you are underwater, count until you surface again. This takes away your panic because generally you are only held underwater for a few seconds.
- If everything gets a bit too much for you, go back to the beach with the next wave riding in the prone position.
- Watch out for the shore break!
- Weighting the tail of the board reduces speed, and weighting the front creates it.
- To surf along a wave, paddle for the wave at an angle.
- Do not give up! Do not give up! Do not give up! And, do not give up!

Not even flying beats the feeling – birds-eye view of Pipeline, Hawaii (Photo by Chiemsee, photographer Erik Aeder)

III. ADVANCED SURFING

By now you will have surfed a few waves, and will have gone through the full washing cycle a few times. You will sometimes have thought that your last moment had come while you were scratching to paddle over a big set of waves and, you will certainly know that one of the worst feelings in this sport is putting on a cold and wet rashguard. You are sitting at home and can think of nothing else but the unbelievable feeling of gliding on a wave. You sit there planning your next surfing trip and places like Hawaii, Australia or Bali are buzzing around in your head. Ah well, obviously you have a severe case of surf fever and you simply cannot shake it off. You better start thinking about how you are going to explain to your girl- or boyfriend that, in the future, there will only be holidays in places that have waves.

In the next chapter we want to go into a few things to do with equipment, describe some manoeuvres for the advanced, give a few tips about how to behave when there are other surfers in the water, and talk a little about the weather, waves and different sea bottoms.

1 What's Next?

So you think you are an advanced surfer, and begin reading this book by starting here. But who is actually an advanced surfer?

Is it the surfer who surfs the Hawaiian winter monster waves, or perhaps the one who knows what the leash is for? It is difficult to say who is and who is not. Therefore, we have tried to compile a few basic requirements that you should at least have.

1.1 Requirements for the Advanced Surfer

The first thing is that you should be a very good swimmer, above all in the ocean. Splashing around in a swimming pool is one thing, but getting back to the beach, swimming between currents and waves after you have snapped your leash, is a completely different story. You should always be able to swim from the line-up through to the beach. A further important requirement is the ability to be able to 'read' the waves a little, so that you can at least tell whether the waves are surfable or not. It is also very important to be able to recognise, from the beach, where there are possible currents running and where there are shallows.

Also you should know something about on what sort of bottom the waves break in the area – for example, whether the bottom is sand or a reef. Attached to this is the ability to judge the size of the waves. This is extremely difficult when there is no other surfer in the water, and you have nothing else to compare the size of the wave with. Viewing from the beach, the waves always appear somewhat smaller than when you are out there lying on your board.

It is even more difficult to assess who is an advanced surfer and who is not from the degree of skill. There are, of course, different opinions about this. But again let's try to find a few basics. An advanced surfer knows how to paddle well i.e., he knows how to lie on the board, and how to catch a wave by paddling with the necessary speed so that the wave actually picks him up. Standing up should not present a challenge any more, and he should be able to surf the unbroken part of a wave diagonally. He should, of course, be able to manage and be able to control the manoeuvres we described in the previous chapter. Let's make this clear – the surfboard should go where you want it to go and not vice versa. Also take-offs should not end up as nose dive most of the time. OK?

But all this is really only the basic – you should not be tempted to think, "No problem, I've stood up twice, I must be what those guys call advanced" – and off you go to Fiji. Realistic judgement of your own ability is surely also a factor defining an advanced surfer.

1.2   Equipment for the Advanced

et's start with the surfboard. There are all types and sizes of surfboards, and by rights each wave calls for a particular sort of board. Big waves need different boards than small waves. Hollow breaking waves call for a different board than those used for flat, mellow rolling waves, and there are different boards for fast breaking waves and slow breaking waves. But of course this can get out of proportion, and since we are not all pro surfers, who get their boards paid for by sponsors, and carry a giant boardbag stuffed with at least ten boards everywhere they go, let us limit this to the basic shapes. Essentially a surfer needs two types of boards – a shortboard for small waves and a gun for more serious ones. These two types of boards will be described in the next section.

Now put your log (we mean your beginner's board) in the corner and jump on a smaller, more manoeuvrable board called a shortboard. Unless, that is, you want to carry on your career as a longboarder.

A shortboard is between 6 and 7 foot long, approximately 16–19 inches wide, and between 2 and 3 inches thick. The selection of the right board depends on your height, your weight, your ability and, last not least, the kind of waves that you are going to use it in. For young people, according to age, size and weight, boards between 5'5" and 6'8" are the most suitable. A grown-up needs a board between 6'1" and 6'10". Heavier and larger surfers should use a slightly longer and thicker board. As an example let's consider a surfer who is about 185 cm tall and weighs around 75-80 kilos. For this surfer, a shortboard upwards from 6'6", about 2.5 inches thick and around about 18 inches wide would be the best option. Please do not take these figures as firm measurements. Even between the pro surfers there are large differences. The American Kelly Slater, for example, surfs mostly with extremely thin and narrow boards, while his Tahitian colleague Vetea "Poto" David uses very thick and wide boards for the same waves. Which board is the right one depends also on your level of skill. Someone who is moving from the beginner status to the advanced will find that with a small, thin board and its inherent low buoyancy, paddling will be made unnecessarily more difficult, and he will not reach the necessary speed. In summary, basically thicker and longer boards, just like the beginner's board, allow easier paddling and make it easier to catch waves because they float better. Shorter, thinner boards are generally more manoeuvrable and are easy to duck-dive with. The bottom line is that it is up to each surfer to find out by trying different sizes and shapes which board he gets on with best.

Returning to the shortboards: these are suitable for small to medium sized waves, and because of their shape and weight guarantee maximum manoeuvrability (and fun). Now, to the secret love affair of all surfers – the gun. Simply at the mention of the word gun, one immediately starts dreaming of large waves, adrenaline surges as the horizon grows darker and a giant set rolls in. If only you could take your gun to bed with you every night (we heard some funny stories though). OK, OK, enough of this – but what is a gun? It is a long, narrow board that is mainly used for surfing in large and/or hollow waves. Its size is between 7 to 10 feet. It is approximately 17.5 to 20 inches wide and between 2.25 and 3.75 inches thick.

On the one hand, the length allows the surfer to catch large and steep waves more easily, and on the other hand it provides him with the necessary stability needed when surfing at a higher speed and helps him cope with larger chops on the face of some waves. The thickness of the board additionally supports this. Do not think that larger and/or steeper waves would be easier to catch; It is quite the opposite. Especially here, because of the higher speed at which the waves are travelling, the surfer has to paddle extremely hard to catch the wave. More about this later. If you consider that in big waves the surfer paddles perhaps 90% and surfs for 10% of his time, it is obvious that the gun has to be a good paddler and needs more buoyancy than a shortboard. Another important point is the confidence a gun gives in large waves. You can trust your gun that it will safely guide you down the wave and bring you back to the beach. So the gun is not only good for surfing big waves, it will also put you in the right state of mind. It is not simply only an extended shortboard. Generally there are two sorts of shapes for a gun – the conventional shape and the modern shape. The conventionally shaped gun is built to surf the classic Big-Wave style: take-off, drop down the face without wiping-out and a long solid bottom turn. Modern shaped guns are narrower and thinner giving the board additional manoeuvrability. A modern shaped gun is exactly the right choice for an average to good surfer.

Most of today's guns have a so-called "pintail" i.e., it tapers to a point at the end of the board. How pointed a pintail should be, depends on the waves where it will be ridden. For example, in Hawaii, some people who surf at Waimea and Sunset (both are places on the north shore of the island of Oahu), use extremely pointed pintails, that both ends of the board look almost identically pointed. Sometimes the tail is even more pointed than the nose. A board like this, however, will only go straight. These enormous boards are called "rhino chasers". The name stems from a remark made by Big-Wave legend Pat Curren (Tom Curren's father and the famous shaper of the Waimea Redwood/Balsa gun), who said something like, "You do not go hunting rhinos with a double-barreled gun. If you're going to hunt big waves take a big gun." The length of a gun depends on where it is going to be used. Rhino chasers, about 10 feet long, are used for waves in places such as Waimea, Sunset, Todos Santos (Baja California, Mexico) or Mavericks (California). In Europe you would only need a gun no longer than 8 feet, unless that is you are going to surf either in France in winter, when the Atlantic storms are raging, or you want to catch a giant swell off the Canaries. So, as you can see, there are endless different shapes and lengths of shortboards and guns. When you buy you should watch out for the following points: tail, rocker, rails, stringer etc. So let's take a closer look.

Tail: The term tail refers to the rear end (stern) of the surfboard. Today's shortboards essentially use two types of tails. One is called the "square tail". It almost appears as if it has been squarely cut off at the end. According to how far it is rounded at the end, it is also called a "rounded square tail". A board with a square tail is very responsive and is therefore best suited for radical manoeuvres in small waves. If you surf mainly beachbreaks, you should get a board with a square tail. Please do not mistake us. We have experienced beachbreak waves in France (e.g., in Hossegor) that could take on any wave seen in Hawaii (of course on an "off" day). All in all, you will find small to medium-sized waves on the average beachbreak in France, California or elsewhere ranging between 2 to 6 foot. Just perfect to have a bit of fun. A board with a square tail will be the right choice here.

The other popular type of tail is called a "pintail" which we have already mentioned. Similarly to the square tail, a pintail that has been rounded is called just that – a "rounded pintail". The pintail is mostly used in connection with the gun shapes. Of course, there are shortboards with a pintail. Such a board is only practical if you are mainly surfing fast, hollow waves in the 4-6 foot range, like those found for example in Kirra (Queensland, Australia) or Mundacca (in the Basque country, Northern Spain).

Shortboard
6'5" long with a rounded square tail, nose lift (note upward pointing shape from the shadow), stringer and full-deck (Photo: Menges/Diel)

A pintail is more difficult to turn, but has the advantage of giving the board more stability when surfing at higher speed. The tail does not break away as easily because it cuts deeper into the water.

Finally, perhaps the "swallow tail" is worth a mention. It literally looks like the tail of a swallow at the rear. The shapers used this type of tail a lot in the 1970's, and today is often found in specific shaped boards e.g., the so-called "fish".

Fins: Most modern shortboards and guns have three fins, and are called a "thruster". The thruster was introduced by the Australian Simon Anderson in 1980. The two outside fins are positioned approximately 1 foot from the tail of the board and about 1 inch in from the rails. The third fin is placed directly in the middle of the board and is about 4 inches away from the tail. The advantage of the thruster is that one fin is always in the water, even during a radical turn. As a result the tail will not break away (unless you do a tail slide manoeuvre on purpose). The thruster makes it possible for the surfer to gain additional acceleration coming out of fast turns such as, for example, the bottom turn. There are also boards with other numbers of fins. As an example, a single fin is sometimes used on a gun with a very pointed pintail.

As we have mentioned before these boards are used for steep, very fast waves. Boards with two (made famous by four time world champion Mark Richards) or four fins (called a "quad") are not seen so much these days. Very practical, particularly while you are travelling, are fin systems that allow you to remove the fins. Those, who have ever experienced the misery of unpacking their boards after a flight with perfect waves waiting just outside the front door – only to find the fins broken off, have particularly welcomed the introduction of these systems.

A further advantage is that you can fit different types of fins to play around and experiment with. You must still take care when putting in and taking off the fins from the board. It is very easy to damage the board when trying to force a fin in or out of its slot. Several different systems have been developed but are far away from being perfect. As every system has its pros and cons, it is best that you choose the system with which you feel most comfortable.

Thruster with a rounded square tail, hard rails and removable fins (Photo: Menges/Diel)

Rail: The surfboard's rails are defined by the degree of their rounded edges. 'Soft', smoothly shaped rails, running from the upper side to the bottom, are well suitable for the beginner. A board with soft rails is easy to turn. Advanced surfers, however, would be better off choosing a board with 'hard' rails. The edges are smoothly rounded off on the upper side and at the bottom there are clearly defined edges. These dig deep into the water and thereby give a better grip on the wave than the soft rails. They have an advantage on steep wave faces when, after the take-off, the edge digs into the water and despite the steepness the board maintains a grip. With soft rails there is always a danger that the board will break away and slips sideways. This is a similar effect to skiing with badly honed edges on your skis.

Rocker: The term 'rocker' describes the surfboard's bottom longitudinal curve, from the tail to the nose. However, often only the curve at the nose – the so-called 'nose lift' – is what is meant. Generally speaking, each shortboard and gun should have a lifted-up nose. This is determined by the form of the more hollow breaking waves which usually have somewhat of an edge at the bottom. If the nose of the board did not have the lift, then the tip would always dig into the water at this edge. Furthermore, the more overall rocker the board has the more the board gains in manoeuvrability. If the rocker is too fierce the board will push water in front of it and slow you down. Different surfers prefer different shapes of rockers. If possible, you should try out the different rocker-shapes to see which one suits you best.

Stringer: The stringer is a thin strip of wood that runs down the centre of the board. This gives the board strength and rigidity and lessens the danger of it breaking. Guns often have a thicker stringer than shortboards because they are stressed more in bigger waves.

Despite the fact that the stringer is only very thin it gives the necessary strength. If it is damaged or split anywhere along its length, the board will be extremely unstable, and it will probably break in half the next time you stand on it. You should make sure that the stringer is alright when you are buying a board.

These are some of the more important terms used, and are those that you will need when buying a board. Before you buy a board pick it up under the arm. You must get the feel of its shape and rails. This will tell you whether this board is the right one for you or not. You can also have one made especially for you. This is a so-called 'custom-made board'. However this may take some time and depends on the shaper and his workload. Let's say you want a genuine Rusty Preisendorfer, Glenn Minami or a Phil Byrne, then you might have to wait a few weeks.

If you use a relatively unknown shaper then it will usually be quicker. The big advantage of custom-made boards is that the board will be made exactly to your own requirements. You can tell the shaper what your surfing ability is (being truthful here really pays off), and where you want to use the board. If you are able to, you can tell him your preferences for thickness, width and length, as well as the kind of tail and rocker. Last but not least, you can choose your own design.

For the advanced surfer, the following accessories should also get a mention:

Grip deck: A grip deck or a pad is glued on to the surfboard to give the surfer a good grip on his board without using wax. There are grip decks for the tail only as well as so-called 'full decks' which usually come in two pieces. The second piece is stuck in the middle of the board. Some decks have a slight rise on the tail pad, called a 'kick'. This allows the surfer to apply even more pressure on the tail, and prevents the foot from slipping off the back of the board during radical manoeuvres. The disadvantage of many of the decks, up until now, has been that when you surfed without a wetsuit you easily got a rash because they were rather rough. New developments like Powderkeg or Kgrip, for example, use different materials to prevent a rash without diminishing the grip qualities. There are a number of different decks on the market that are recommended by various pro surfers. It is difficult to say which is the best. One of the disadvantages with almost all the decks, however, is that when you are surfing with surf boots, sometimes you feel as if your feet are glued to the board as well. It is then difficult to adjust your foot position while surfing.

Helmet: Surfers use a helmet mainly when the waves break over a reef or rocks in extremely shallow water. A helmet can also offer some protection against the sun. At the moment there is only one company

making these in two models. The company Gath has one helmet with a
visor and one without. The visor is good to protect the eyes against the
glaring sun.

Finally, a mention of the **leash** and **boots.** A normal leash for a
shortboard is about 4-6 feet long. For the gun you should buy a longer
leash, about 8 feet long. In large waves the leash is subjected to a
greater strain, and therefore has to be a little stronger. If the leash gets
caught up on a rock or gets stuck between coral, you must be able to
undo it with one movement of the hand. You must know how to remove
quickly the leash because if you are stuck underwater after a wipe-out,
you do not have time to start thinking about how to open the leash.
Many leashes have a little flap that opens it in one pull. When we were
in Hawaii for the first time, and we asked the local behind the counter
what the little flap was for, he looked at us with a big smile, pulled it
open and said, "Cos you do not die." So have a good look at your leash.
You should have at least one pair of surf boots, even if you do not intend
to surf in ice-cold water. They will protect you from reefs and sea urchins.
On some beaches you have to walk across a reef to get to the water.
Without boots, this is just about impossible. The soles of the shoes
should not be as thick as the rubber on diving shoes or those used by
windsurfers, as you would loose the feel for the board.

1.3   The Surf Code

*T*hose of you, who do not have their own private wave directly in
front of their front door must learn the surf code as well as a few
unwritten rules by heart, before paddling out between other surfers
somewhere in the world. First of all the most important of all the rules –
the right of way. Basically the surfer who is on the inside, nearest to the
point where the wave is breaking (the white water), has the right of way.
A surfer who takes-off into a wave, but is further away from another

surfer who has already started closer to the break and has started at the same time, has to kick out and leave the wave. To interfere with the right of way of another surfer is called a 'drop-in'. The surfer, about to start must always watch out whether there is someone taking-off on the inside. Besides the resulting arguments, a drop-in is often the cause of an injury or a broken board. One exception to this rule is when a surfer has caught a wave further out and is surfing past a surfer waiting to catch a wave. If the waiting surfer, who is now practically behind the other, starts into the wave, he is actually nearer to the breaking point of the wave and thus would have the right of way. In this case however, the surfer who stood up first has the right of way. This ruling often leads to disagreements in the water.

Sorry!
(Photo: Joli)

A further important rule is that the surfer who is riding a wave has the right of way over another surfer paddling out. This means that in some cases the one paddling out must necessarily paddle into the white water foam instead of safely going over the shoulder of the wave as that is where the surfer is also aiming at. This can be quite tough especially in bigger waves. Who would not want to slip over the shoulder of a big incoming wave and not have the next one break on top of him? Let's summarise this:

The surfer who is already up and riding on a wave or who is closer to the breaking point of the wave on the take-off has absolute priority.

Someone surfing has priority over someone paddling out.

Now a few words about the unwritten rules. If you are paddling out and a broken wave is rolling towards you, do not throw your board away and bail out but always at least hold on to your board and try to duck-dive through – that is unless you really fear for your life as a monster wave is breaking right on top of you. The surfer behind you, who gets your board smashed into his face, or the one surfing the wave who may collide with your loose board, will not exactly become your best friend. Equally something you should avoid is to push your board off in front of you into the wave if you have to abort your take-off for whatever reason. If there is a surfer already on the wave he will get the board smashed straight onto his head.

If you are surfing on a beach where the waves are breaking left and right (a so-called peak), you should call out to any other surfer about to start at the same time as yourself, to indicate to him which way you want to go.

Something that creates a bad atmosphere is when a surfer constantly tries to paddle on the inside to get the priority. In other words, imagine you are sitting out in the water waiting for a wave. The

The boogie boarder has started further inside and has priority.
(Photo: Joli)

surfer next to you is sitting actually closer to the anticipated point of break (he is sitting on your inside). When the wave rolls in, you quickly paddle round him to get on his inside and gain priority, or even worse, paddle in front of him so that he cannot paddle for the wave. This latter bad behaviour is called "to snake" someone.

One of the most important unwritten rules is to respect the locals. Remember they have been surfing there every day for years. Localism has figured as a much-discussed topic in surfing magazines over the last few years. You might have read about fights in the water, broken surfboards, cars being broken into etc. On La Réunion (Indian Ocean) we once saw a boogie-boarder draw a knife and attack an Australian surfer because he had dropped into the wave in front of him. Certain beaches such as Oxnard in California or the Westside on Oahu (Hawaii) are well-renowned for such incidents. Most of the time the arguments start because a surfer shows disrespect for the rules and/or for the locals. Respect means always leave some waves for the locals and do not paddle on the inside right away.

However, to put a few things in perspective: naturally you should not just sit there and let everyone go past you. Use your skills and try hard to catch a wave. do not insist on your right of way and never fight for a wave. Nothing looks more ridiculous than seeing two people trying to fight in the water, and half drowning themselves in the process. Another important rule to avoid trouble in the water is quite simple. Do not be an idiot! One can only express this li ke this, because there are some surfers who think they can do anything and everything. These people simply attract trouble! Apart from this, a good surfer should not need to steal the right of way from others, because he will catch enough waves anyway.

Nevertheless, localism is not as bad as it sometimes sounds. We, personally, have never had any serious trouble with the locals anywhere in the world apart from the odd little abuse.

1.4   The Duck-dive

Yes, the duck-dive indeed! Probably, this is one of the most important things that you have to master, otherwise you will never get out over the white water and into the real line-up. If you have seen the film "North Shore", then you will probably know what you have to do. In case you have not then write this down "You have to dive like a duck if you want to surf on the North Shore". Sounds a bit funny, and you do not have to duck-dive along most of the North Shore anyway to get out. However, there is some truth in the matter.

One of the secrets of duck-diving is your paddling speed. The individual sequence of movements can be described as follows. A wave, that has already broken, or is about to break, is rolling towards you. You paddle up to it at maximum speed. At the last moment, you press the front of the board under the water, by doing a kind of a push-up. The wave is now right over you, but the tail is still out of the water. Now you press the tail down with your knee or your foot. You will have to try this out to discover whether you find it easier with the knee or the foot. You can actually press down harder with your foot, thus pushing the board deeper under the surface of the water. This will give you an advantage in larger waves. You can use the other leg as a kind of rudder when the wave vibrates over you under water. For a short moment, your whole body is now under the water. You dive, so to speak, underneath the wave. The speed reached in paddling gives you the necessary momentum to dive through under the wave. On the other side you bob up like a duck out of the water. It is important that the duck-dive is carried out in a flowing motion. Pushing the front and the tail down should happen at almost the same moment. You have to set up the duck-dive so that both you and the board dive underneath at just the moment that you reach the wave or as it breaks over you. Because of the board's natural buoyancy you will only be able to dive for a short time; thus timing is of vital importance. The more volume your board has the more difficult the duck-dive will be.

Tip:

Keep the eyes open in clear water so that you can see how the wave is passing over you. This way you can get a feeling for when you have to surface again. A good duck-dive is difficult and requires a lot of practice. There are some surfers, who even after several years still have not managed to master it. As a result they get pushed back after every wave. So, keep working on your duck-diving techniques.

The sequence of the duck-dive:
(Drawings: Stefan "Muli" Müller)

1)  2)

- Paddle strongly towards the wave or the white water.

- Shortly before the wave hits you, push the nose of the board deep down into the water with both hands.

- Directly afterwards push the tail under the water with the foot or the knee.

4)  5)

- Under water, give the board a push forward with your arms.

- Surface and straight away begin to paddle (the next wave is already waiting).

2   How are Waves Created?

No doubt, waves are the most important thing that a surfer needs. They are the reason why he is always travelling round the world hoping to find, somewhere, the perfect wave. A surfer has to know how and why waves are created, where they come from and in which direction they spread out. He has to understand how the moon and the tide influence the waves, and how a sandbank, reef or submerged rocks affect the way in which the waves break. Being able to read a weather map helps the surfer to recognise a possible swell. Of course, you can use surf reports, or by using (we will not say surfing) the Internet, read weather forecasts and reports on wave heights, as well as see live pictures of surfing spots. Nevertheless, every surfer should know what those little circles on the weather map are all about.

Empty Tube in Indonesia (Photo: Menges / Diel)

Naturally we do not want to start a lecture on weather forecasts here, and it is almost certain that the next piece will be somewhat dry for you to read. However, we think that every surfer should have some basic knowledge of the connection between weather and waves.

2.1   Weather

What do all the circles and figures mean on the weather chart? Why does a depression or a low bring waves and a high-pressure zone does not?

The sun's rays heat the earth. Layers of air are warmed up and rise. Cold air streams in to take its place. The rotation of the earth moves the air around and airstreams are created.

When warm airstreams meet cold ones turbulence occurs. The cold airstream pushes itself under the warm one and heat and energy is released with the result that the clouds and air circulate. This is how a storm begins, circulating counter-clockwise in the Northern Hemisphere, and clockwise in the Southern Hemisphere. On the weather chart you will find so-called "isobars". These define areas with the same air pressure and are measured in millibars.

The numbers on the isobars tell you how high or how low the pressure is in the particular area. They are measured in relation to sea level. Wind is created when the airstream from a depression, and a high-pressure area, equal each other out. The direction of the airstream flows from the area of high pressure to areas of low pressure.

The surfers favourite picture of the weather chart is a depression where the isobars are close to each other and under 1,000 millibars in the centre of it. Such a depression will bring waves if it is moving in the right direction. The best waves are created by tropical storms such as cyclones, typhoons or hurricanes – basically these are all terms for one and the same thing: a storm depression. However you want to call them, one thing is for sure – they create waves.

There are numerous weather conditions in the world that can produce a good swell. However, it would be well beyond the scope of this book to cover the ideal weather situations on all the world's seas; you would probably fall asleep anyway.

At this point let's take a short look at the subject of winds near the coastline. Generally, one can say that the wind close to the coastline will always blow in the direction of the warmer area. During the day the land is warmed up by the sun to such a degree that the wind will blow from the sea to cool it down – a so-called "onshore". During the night the land slowly cools down and the wind backs round to blow in the direction of the warmer sea. This is why most beaches have an "offshore" wind early in the morning. This wind usually turns round at about midday. The offshore

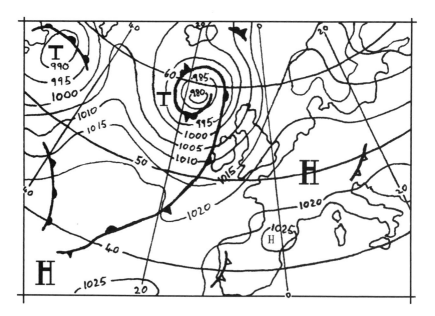

Ideal weather conditions for perfect waves on the Atlantic coast. Pack your boards on the roof rack (Drawing: Stefan "Muli" Müller)

blows against the waves slowing them down but smoothing the surface. Thus the wave will break cleaner and with more perfection. Paddling for a wave will be made more difficult, and you will have to give a couple or so extra strokes if you want to catch it.

Sometimes you will not even be able to see the wave you are trying to take-off on because of all the spray created by the offshore wind. Contrary to this, an onshore wind causes the waves to break earlier and the surface of the water will be choppy. Both not ideal for surfing. Perfect conditions are sometimes met when, just before the wind turns around, there is a stillness with no wind at all. The water is then quite smooth. These conditions are called "glassy". Therefore always remember the old saying the early 'board' catches the 'tube' or something like that! The morning session – dawn patrol – is therefore often the best session of the whole day.

The Life-cycle of a Wave

Waves are produced by storms far out to sea. The water is set in motion by the storm. When the surface begins to ripple and becomes turbulent, one speaks of a "chop" or "wind chop". If the chop gets larger, gradually a swell is formed. At the beginning the waves, whipped up by the storm, are unstructured and move in all directions. A real swell is only formed from the rippling of the waves when the storm begins to back off. The swell then begins to move towards the coast. Such a swell is often referred to as a "groundswell". The waves often travel thousands of kilometres. When they break on a beach they will have lost some height and the gap between the waves will be longer, dependent on where they stem from and how far the swell has come. Generally big waves move faster than small ones. They often come in "sets" i.e., groups of 3-9 waves at once. A short pause follows each set.

These pauses are used by surfers to paddle out. The type of swell that every surfer longs for is created by a groundswell, where the waves come in regular groups, with no wind blowing as they break onto the beach. Quite the opposite is a so-called "windswell". The water is churned up by strong winds near the coast and the ocean often looks as if someone had dumped a ton or two of washing detergent in it. Further out to sea the surface is covered with white crests. These conditions are called "blown out", and unfortunately happen far too often.

The Tide

The tide also plays a role in the creation of a wave. Tide is the product of the simultaneous force of attraction of the sun and the moon, as well as the gravitational pull of the earth. One differentiates the tide as either a low tide or a high tide.

Low tide and high tide change on a six hourly rhythm and make a time jump of about an hour each day. A useful aid to the surfer is the so-called tide table or tide chart for each beach, or the whole coastline. These will tell you exactly the time of low or high tide. The tables also give you coefficients for each day expressing the difference between the low and high tide. Surfers look for so-called "King tides", which are tides with extreme differences between high and low tide, and have very high coefficients. Tide charts can usually be found in a local surf shop. If there are no surf shops you can find the timings in the local newspaper, and simply add an hour for the timings for the next day. You can also ask locals or the fishermen. They usually know the best.

Low and high tides have a great influence on a surfing spot. If a swell is building the waves will increase with the incoming high tide. The opposite occurs with an outgoing low tide where the waves may get smaller but generally steeper as they will break in shallower water. This is, of course, very dependent on the type of beach. You should always know whether the tide is going out or coming in. At some surfing spots not knowing can be dangerous. For example, waves breaking over a reef, which can normally be surfed without problems during a high tide, will be steeper, and will be breaking in shallow receding water (if there is any left at all). A wipe-out in the shallows over a razor-sharp reef can cause nasty injuries. In the Cook Islands in the South Pacific, for example, you surf only on the incoming high tide. The waves break over passages in the coral reef, which encircle the island. At low tide the water lying in lagoons inside the ring of the coral reef is sucked out. It can be almost impossible to get back through these passages, as the current is far too strong. Surfing over the almost dry reef, you will get yourself back in to the inside of the lagoon for sure, but you would not do your surfboard any favours and you may end up with a reef cut or two yourself.

2.2 How Do I Read the Surf spot?

You know the story. "Come on, let's go back to the other beach. The waves are much better there – Or shall we stay here? There's a good channel where we can paddle out, or ..." and so on and so forth. We are talking about the surf check. It belongs to surfing as much as paddling out does. Many of those who we have taught to surf could often never understand what was so important about the surf check. This is where you just sit there looking at the ocean quietly, watching a few sets come in, before you enter the water. Knowledge of the surf spot, its bottom and the currents, is often the deciding factor between fun and frustration. You have to learn to 'read' the surf spot. Every surfer must have some idea of what is waiting for him out there. "Let's paddle out, and then have a look" can often end up with an unpleasant surprise. Naturally, a surf check on a beach break is not quite so important as on a reef in Indonesia. Nevertheless a beach break has its own obstacles in the form of strong currents between the sandbanks, and tricky shore breaks.

Surf check at Sunset Beach Hawaii (Photo: Ecki Hillebrecht)

In the following section we want to go into some of the different types of bottoms and the influence these have on how a wave breaks.

It is common on all beaches that the wave meets the bottom of the ocean, and pushes its energy up in the direction of its crest, causing it to break. The way the wave now breaks depends on the bottom and its shape, and that is what we want to have a closer look at.

The Beachbreak

The "beach break" is the simplest and least dangerous form of a break. The bottom consists of sand, which underwater more or less gradually rises. The wave breaks either on an offshore sandbank or directly onto the beach. However, whether a beach break is surfable depends on how steep the beach rises, and at which point on it the wave breaks. If the bottom rises up steeply, and if the wave breaks as a shore break, crashing directly onto the beach, you risk a broken board rather than a surfing experience.

Best for surfing are the beaches where the waves break on offshore sandbanks. These are often found near stone piers, rivermouths or harbour walls, but of course they can also be found on open beaches. Around sandbanks there are currents. On open beaches a current runs between the beach and the sandbank. Strong currents between sandbanks stream out to sea. These are proportionally stronger the narrower the underwater channel between them is. The current is created when the water, pushed over the sandbank by the waves, tries to find its own way back out. The surfer can use this current almost as a conveyor to carry him out to the line-up. Near to harbour walls or piers the current often runs directly along the side of these, and again the surfer can use them to his advantage.

A beach break usually provides a simple, short ride. The waves roll softly in towards the beach. Parts of the wave crest move faster than the rest. However, if the wave breaks along its whole length, this is called a "close-out", and often a take-off is all you will get before the wave closes down. The biggest disadvantage of beach breaks is their unpredictability – i.e., the line-up is not clearly defined and it is hard to tell where the waves will actually break. Another drawback is the often insurmountable mass of white water that you have to duck-dive through to get out, as well as the increasing number of close-out waves as the swell gets bigger.

Nevertheless, not all beachbreaks gently roll off as described above. There are also breaks which literally suck up the water from the sandbanks to form a hollow tube. These waves break top-to-bottom, i.e., the lip of the wave breaks directly into the base of the wave. Typically reef waves break top-to-bottom. There are, however, several world-class waves that break onto a sandy bottom and have this top-to-bottom characteristic. Puerto Escondido in Mexico – the Mexican pipeline – is an example. The sand is so hard there that the waves break onto it as if on a reef. Other top-to-bottom beachbreaks are Hossegor (France), Duranbah (Australia) – and the list goes on.

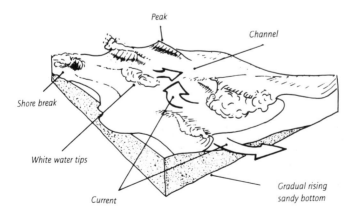

Peak
Channel
Shore break
White water tips
Current
Gradual rising sandy bottom

A gradual rising beachbreak with various peaks and currents (Drawing: Stefan "Muli" Müller)

Reef Break

The most spectacular and beautiful waves in the world break on reefs. The depth of the water varies to extremes. The wave often breaks quite far out from the shore, but in spite of this, the waves break in dangerously flat water. Reefs rise up steeply, and so the wave hits it without being slowed down by a gradually rising ocean floor. The result is that the wave's energy is transformed immediately into height and lifts the wave upwards almost like a wall out of the water. Sometimes it appears as if there is no swell, and suddenly a steep green wall stands up in front of you. On riffs waves break steep, hollow and top-to-bottom. The lip of the wave pitches forward and forms a tube. Take-offs on reefs can be extremely difficult because the waves break so quick and hollow – more about this in Chapter 3.1 "Surfing Hollow Waves". The reef can be either a rocky, volcano or coral one. The advantage of reef breaks is that you can tell exactly where the waves will break. The wave can be assessed with some certainty because it always breaks at the same point. Around the reef the water is deeper and no waves break there. The surfer is able to paddle around behind the breakline easily.

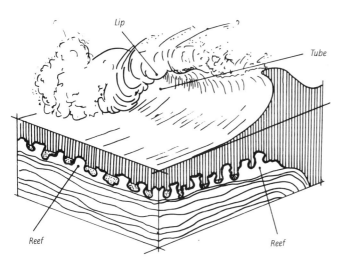

Lip

Tube

Reef

Reef

Hollow steep top-to-bottom wave breaking on to a reef bottom (Drawing: Stefan "Muli" Müller)

In Fiji or Indonesia, this can be rather extreme. The boats, that take you out to the reefs can anchor 10-20 metres away from absolutely huge waves, while the local captain is nonchalantly snoozing because he knows that he is sitting in safe waters.

It is a great feeling to surf in clear water over a coral reef. But everything has its price. Coral reefs are often as sharp as a razor, and infested with sea urchins. Wipe-outs can be quite nasty. Surfing on reefs is only for the expert. So, if you have difficulties to make the take-off on a hollow wave – leave it alone! Boots and a helmet are often necessary. Just remember – coral is a living organism. If you cut yourself, there is always the danger of a painful infection when particles get stuck in the wound. This is why, on our travels, we always carried a toothbrush and disinfectant to brush the wound absolutely clean. A bit painful, but very effective. You will learn to respect this method if you find your whole leg, or some other part of the body, swollen and puffy after receiving only a little scratch. Surfing on reefs is breathtaking and exciting, but dangerous. Some of the best reef breaks are Pipeline (North Shore, Oahu, Hawaii), Cloudbreak (Fiji), Uluwatu (Bali, Indonesia) and G-Land (Java, Indonesia).

Point Break

In a "point break", it is not only the bottom that causes the wave to break. The main characteristic of a point break is a headland (or point) that reaches out into the sea. The wave's energy concentrates itself against the tip of the headland. Here the wave starts to break and runs along parallel to the land. The point break delivers the longest rides of all. At a point break you can take-off in several places. The main take-off zone is usually at the spot where the wave first meets the headland. This makes the take-off difficult, above all when there are lots of surfers in the water. As you are often surfing parallel and quite close to a rock-lined headland a point break can be dangerous. If you wipe-out directly after the take-off it is quite easy to get washed into the rocks. Some of the most well-known point breaks are Kirra (Australia), Jeffrey's Bay (South Africa) and Rincon (California).

The speed and power with which a swell arrives on a beach, reef or point depends on whether the wave breaks on the mainland or on an island. Waves that break on islands such as Hawaii, Fiji or Tahiti are faster and have significantly more power than waves breaking on mainland shores such as France or California. Most of the Pacific islands have volcanic origins. They rise up out of the water steeply, and the waves do not lose speed as they meet the island shores. Waves travelling over the undersea continental shelves soon lose some of their power and speed before they finally reach the mainland shores. There are some exceptions like the waves in Hossegor, France. This is because, in the region of Hossegor, the European undersea continental shelf buckles downward braking the waves at a later point.

Well, we have managed to fight our way through that – hard work, eh? At least, you know now (almost) all there is to know about the weather, wind and waves, and you will be able to really annoy your friends with all your smart comments on the next surfari. So, you do know it all n'est-ce-pas? OK, once again, slowly: an isobar is ... That's enough!!!

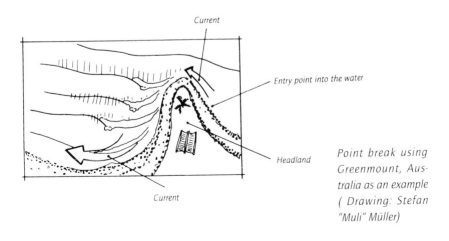

Current

Entry point into the water

Headland

Current

Point break using Greenmount, Australia as an example (Drawing: Stefan "Muli" Müller)

Serious fun!
(Photo: O'Neill, photographer: Bill Morris)

3 Let's Get Serious!

hat do you mean 'serious'? We just want to have fun. Of course, but part of the fun is the adrenaline rush you get when a monster wave set appears on the horizon; when you paddle for a sucking top-to-bottom wave; when you pull into a tube or when you can see the sharp reef through the water during the take-off. The only real danger of all these things is the reef. Everything else is mainly just buzzing around in your head. By saying 'serious' we do not mean that the fun will stop – quite the contrary. Demanding waves will need skill, concentration and commitment. The following chapter is therefore for everyone, who generally does not fall during the take-off, can surf backhand almost as well as forehand and who is not afraid of waves in the 2-4 feet range.

3.1 Surfing Hollow Waves

hen we talk about a hollow wave we mean waves which break top-to-bottom. The particular thrill of these waves is, on the one hand, the speed at which they break, and thus the speed at which you will ride on them. On the other hand, hollow waves allow you to get a "tube". This is the case when behind the part of the wave which is breaking downward, a sort of pocket or tunnel is formed. A good surfer can ride, depending on the wave, in this tunnel for a few seconds (which will appear like ages once you are in there). From the beach you cannot see the surfer any more. He is actually inside the wave. This manoeuvre rates very high in competitions, and most surfers would agree that getting 'tubed', and to emerge at the end of it, is easily the best feeling in surfing. But to get this far there a few things that you will have to master.

The most critical moment on a hollow wave is the take-off. You will only have a fraction of a second to stand up and get into position on your board. This means that your movements and actions must be perfected.

The first few times that you are confronted with a really hollow wave your heart will probably sink into your boots. You paddle for the wave, and at the moment that you want to stand up the wave is already so steep that you can hardly see the face of it, and you are looking directly down at the bottom of the wave. If you have ever made a drop-in on a skateboard into a halfpipe with a good "vertical", you will know the feeling. It actually feels as if there is no way to make it. But you will be surprised – there is. In addition paddling is often more difficult because of all the water being sucked up by the face of the hollow wave from the bottom. Waves like this are called "sucky waves". This makes it very hard to catch the wave at just the right moment. But this is essential if you want to make the drop. To catch the wave in spite of all this there is only one recipe – paddle hard! The speed of your paddling is crucial. The faster you are, the better. Note the following rule – a hollow wave breaks fast so you must paddle fast to catch it; simple. The steepness of the wave may tempt you to think that it will be easy to catch. Wrong!

It often also helps to paddle additionally with your feet to gain some extra speed in the critical phase before you stand up. In any case, do not forget the two extra arm strokes. In hollow waves it is sometimes better to lie a little forward on the board. The wave is so steep that, when paddling, the nose is lifted up out of the water anyway so it does not dig in so easily. The forward leaning position gives you more downward pressure to overcome the upward sucking motion of the wave. It is worthwhile experimenting a little with your position on the board. Lying further forward also helps if, in addition, an offshore wind is blowing against you. The board sits deeper in the water and gives less resistance to the wind.

A further trick in steep, sucky waves and a strong offshore wind, despite everything we told you, is to relax the overstretched back position and press the chest down onto the board. This way you are slightly pushing the board down the wave. Just try it – it works.

Nice Drop!
(Photo: O'Neill, photographer: Bill Morris)

A further important point is the thoughts that are going through your head. You often paddle for a wave and then pull back from it if you think it is too steep for you. These times are over. Decide beforehand whether you are going to take the wave or not. If It is too big or too steep – OK leave it and let it pass through. If, however, you decide to go for a wave, you must give it all you have got to actually catch it. Never hesitate while you are paddling for a hollow wave. This will mainly lead to you getting stuck in the lip and freefalling down the wave – wipe-out! Paddle and stand up as fast as possible. This is all you should ever think about during the take-off. So, if you paddle for a wave, the decision must have been made whether you are going to take-off on this wave or not.

Now to the drop itself. The important thing is not to surf straight down the wave face with the surfboard lying flat on the surface. Because the wave breaks in a concave form, there is a sharp bend at the bottom of it. The surfboard cannot manage this bend if it sits flat on the surface. The nose digs into the water and someone else rides your tube.

The trick is to surf down the wave at a sideways angle. This way the bottom of your surfboard does not lie flat on the surface but the inside rail holds your surfboard on the wave. The sooner you can press this inside rail into the wave the better. Therefore surf down the wave diagonally from the take-off. Just imagine you are traversing down a steep hill on a snowboard and are riding only on the edge of the board. Thin surfboards have a big advantage. Logically a thin rail cuts in deeper than a thicker one. The board sits deeper in the water and has more stability. At the base of the wave the board will be able to ride much more easily over the bend mentioned earlier. The curvature or rocker of your board matches the bend of the wave. It is essential to apply enough pressure to the inside rail; respectively on the balls of your feet, if you are surfing frontside, and on your heels when you are surfing backside. Some people find it even easier to make the drop backside because they are able to put more pressure on the inside rail by using their heels. Hollow waves often lead to spectacular wipe-outs. Despite all the good advice, you will be late standing up and come unavoidably crashing down the wave. This is all part of it. Make sure that as you fall, you push your board away from you somehow. Water is soft – your board is not. After several freefalls you will soon know how to get to the bottom of the wave. Once you are relatively confident in hollow waves (if you can ever really be so), you will find they are what one metre of fresh powdered snow is for the snowboarder,– the cream on the cake.

When you surf in hollow waves, sooner or later, whether intentionally or unintentionally, you will find yourself in a tube – but what do you do?

Tube Riding

Whether you want to or not, sometime or other you will get into the tube – the barrel – the green room, or whatever you want to call it. If the waves are breaking hollow enough getting into the tube is not a problem. The difficult part is being able to stay on your board and getting out of the tube again. While many a cool Hawaiian would just give a short nonchalant nod after riding a 5-metre wave, he would express his overflowing joy after coming out of the tube with an excited, "yeah", and this is really quite something. Where waves come rolling in through deep waters and suddenly hit a shallow reef the wave does not simply roll out. Instead the lip pitches forward in a big arch. Behind the lip is the pocket, which all surfers seek. If the wave starts to break in relatively deep water, thereby providing an easy entry and take-off, it is not hard to get into the tube when the wave then hits a shallower part of the reef further down the line and pitches. You are already up and riding in a safe stance as the lip pitches. You ride as closely as possible to the wall of the wave, avoiding being thrown off as the lip throws out above you. Additionally flex your knees and bend down to make yourself as small as possible on the board. If you look around now you will find yourself enclosed by the wave for a short moment. You are in the tube. It will then probably go bang and you will again do the full washing cycle as the wave breaks all over you when the tube shuts down. Never mind – let's try once again. What we have described above, getting into the tube automatically is, however, rare. You will have to practice how to get into the tube on purpose. There are two ways of doing this. The first way is to actually slow down to let the breaking wave and the tube catch up with you. This is called a "stall". The second way is to take-off from so far away from the shoulder, i.e., right on the inside, that you can only make the section of the wave that is breaking down in front of you if you drive through it rather than round it. You will

Pull in!
(Photo: Tony King, Surf Travel Co.)

actually surf into the tube from behind it – this is why it is called "to backdoor". The difference between the two techniques is that by stalling you brake to enter the tube, and by backdooring you have to put your foot down to get barreled. Once in the tube everything else is roughly the same.

It is important to keep pressure on the inside rail. It keeps your surfboard on the wave. According to how far you are inside the tube, you have to increase or decrease your speed by slightly changing your position on the board. A little to the front increases your speed, and a little to the rear slows you down. Next time you watch a video of a surfer coming out of the tube, take note of where he is standing on the board (mostly well forward). The stall comes easier when you use your arm or your hand as a brake. When surfing forehand it is your rear hand that drags along the wave to slow you down. In addition this gives you more stability. On your first attempts to get into the tube, it can happen that you will surf in front of it without actually being in it. The only thing to help you here is to move your weight onto the rear foot, and stick your hand into the wave face until the lip catches up with you – then, knock the brakes off and put your foot down again. The problem with these wonderful tubes is that you often receive a decent bashing if you do not make it. This often includes getting bounced on the more or less hard or sharp bottom (remember, you are in shallow water). In spite of all this practice is the only way to learn. That means taking every opportunity to pull into a tube. In small waves this is not such a big thing, but in 6 to 8-footers, with a 2-foot thick lip flying over the top of you, it can be quite intimidating. You will often see a surfer watching his friend surf and encouraging him by shouting, "Pull in"! What this really means is, "do not dodge the tube or you'll be a loser forever." This is why the surfspot "Pipeline" in Hawaii (one of the biggest and most dangerous tubes around) has been given the nickname "The Banzai-Pipeline" after the Japanese Kamikaze pilots' war cry. In order to avoid some of the wipe-outs, at the moment when the situation looks impossible, you can turn hard into the wave face in order to try to break through the back of the wave.

Unfortunately this only works sometimes. If you fall off inside the tube, it is important that you somehow get away from your board. The best way to do this is to do a dive head first forwards and parallel to the wave at the last moment. You can also fall off the back of the board pushing it away with your feet. The wave will still eat you, but you will at least have a greater chance of not hitting your board. One thing to remember, if you jump off, jump in parallel to the wave – and not in the direction of the beach!

Getting tubed on your backhand is a particular challenge. The trick here is to do a so–called "pig-dog". Standing sideways on your board with your back to the wave you will stall by turning your forward (in relation to the tip of your board) shoulder back, and, using the arm belonging to it, drag your hand in the water. At the same time your rear hand grips the outside rail. Now look at yourself and you will know what a 'pig-dog' looks like.

Pig-dog tube on the backhand (Photo: O'Neill, photographer: Bill Morris)

The advantage of this stance is that you can shift your weight back and forth without losing your balance. Additionally grabbing the rail gives you greater stability in steep waves and will automatically make you bend down to fit the tube. It is better to practice this movement a few times on the beach so that in the water you do not have to think too much about it. The key to making a backhand-tube-ride is really the forward shoulder. So, do yourself a favour and pull it back. Once again after me: regulars turn the left shoulder to the rear and grip the rail with the right hand. Goofys do the opposite; turn the right shoulder and grip with the left hand. Only a few surfers can ride a tube backside without pig-dogging. This is then called, however, a "no-hands tube".

Finally the most important tip of all: keep your eyes open inside the tube! First of all it looks really wild inside the tube, and secondly you must look for the light at the end of the tunnel. As long as you can see the exit (sometimes even further away), there is a chance that you will make it through. Pull in!

3.2   Surfing Big Waves

Defining "big waves" already gives us a problem. What is big? What is small? Here is an example. When we were in Australia surfing big waves, as far as we were concerned, we felt like excited children after each of us had surfed a few waves, and had arrived back on the beach safe and sound to tell of our heroic efforts on the high seas. We were sure that we had surfed some absolutely gigantic mountains, but our Australian friend Pete only remarked: "Naah mate, that wasn't even six foot." What, they were only six feet! When we were in the water we had the feeling that we were paddling around between floating houses. Well, that is the thing with wave heights. It is all very subjective, and wave heights are described differently from country to country. It is also quite common, all over the world by the way, to understate modestly when someone is watching and to grossly overexaggerate when no-one is. The kings of understatement are quite definitely the Hawaiians. They calculate practically one to one – metre for foot. This means that conditions upwards of 8 "Hawaiian" feet are not for the faint-hearted. When a Hawaiian surf report tells you that Sunset beach is breaking at 8 to 10 feet, it will be better for you to take your camera and a sun hat to the beach and leave your surfboard at home. Guaranteed, the waves will be bigger than anything you have ever surfed or even seen before. There is something like an unwritten guide to wave sizes though, which gives you a little understanding and the ability to judge surf and wave reports anywhere you are. The waves are measured in feet, however it is not about measuring exact wave heights, but more a question of putting waves into a category. "And the nominees are ..."

- Up to 2 feet: not real waves, but always better than sitting around on the beach.

- Up to 4 feet: small waves, lots of fun.

- 4 feet: ideal fun waves to practice manoeuvres and for a relaxed surfing session.

- 5 feet: more fun than serious, but some adrenaline.

- 6 feet: lots of adrenaline! do not underestimate them, 6-footers are already quite big and powerful– bring a bigger board.

- 6 to 8 feet: (there is not such a thing as a 7-footer), the same as 6-foot but watch out for larger sets, little guns, now and again you will be scared.

- 8 feet: really intensive waves – big waves – think carefully whether you should go out. Your heart is already beating fast while you are still on the beach, just wait until you are in the water. Sets will send everybody scrabbling for the horizon.

- 8 or 10 feet: (once again – no such thing as a nine-footer) If you are a good surfer and do not have any problems with 6-foot waves, put your fear aside, paddle out and try to make it safely but full of adrenaline back to the beach.

- 10 feet: this is the ultimate for most average surfers. If conditions are clean, i.e., smooth water surface, well co-ordinated sets, clearly defined line-ups and no waves higher than 10 feet, you can paddle out and have a look around. Decide for yourself whether to take a wave; a large board is imperative. "do not get caught inside" – which means: do not get caught by large sets. This is because the impact zone – where the lip comes crashing down – will be really serious and dangerous. It is no crime if you do not catch a wave!

Pipeline, Hawaii somewhere around 12-foot (Photo: Kuta Lines Australia)

Without wanting to play things down we could actually stop here, because to be truthful, for most there are very few opportunities of ever surfing anything bigger than 10-foot very successfully. Never mind! 10-foot waves are quite sufficient to be able to tell a story or two to your grandchildren sometime or other – the waves in your story will automatically grow in size over the years anyway.

10 foot and over can really be life-threatening depending on which bottom they break – so no misjudged heroics! The adrenaline factor will be multiplied several times if the waves are breaking top-to-bottom. If they also break on a reef it will already get quite interesting from 4 feet upwards.

From around 18 feet plus, a fully different world begins. There is only a very extreme group of surfers who successfully ride those 20-foot mountains. Even some surfers on the pro-tour do not bother trying to ride such monsters. This is a surfing league on its own. Also there are very few surfing spots in the world where you can surf waves of that size at all. Even in Hawaii there are perhaps only three to four surfspots which can handle this size.

The best known big wave spots around the world are: Waimea Bay and Jaws (Hawaii), Todos Santos (Mexico), Mavericks (California) and Margret River (Australia). Have a look at theses waves on video or in real life from the beach. However, it should not be your aim to have a go at them. This would be rather unrealistic and too frustrating.

So this is why we want to talk about waves between 5 and 10 feet in the following sections. For some, angst will set in a little earlier, and for others a little later. Generally, however, anything above 6 feet deserves some respect.

There are a few things that are vital to enjoy riding big waves:

1. A surfboard around 7 foot long.
2. A strong and longer (than normal) leash.
3. You must be able to duck-dive well – confronted with 5-foot wave breaking in front of you, you do not bail out, instead pull off your absolutely best duck-dive.
4. You need to be in good shape.
5. You feel at home and have no fear in 4 to 5-foot waves.

Got your board waxed? – Then let's go! But just a moment – the surf check – more important then ever.

It is extremely important to know whether boomer-sets (larger than the average size on that day) are coming through in regular intervals or not. They are no problem as long as you recognise them early enough as they appear on the horizon. This will only be possible if you maintain a constant lookout for the sets. When you spot them in time you must know which way to paddle to get out of their way. It is often better not to head straight out, but additionally to cut across diagonally to reach an existing channel that is hopefully there.

Before choosing a wave it is important to know whether you should ride it all the way, or whether you will have to exit prematurely out of the back of it. In big waves it often happens that after the euphoria of making the drop, or perhaps getting a tube, you will want to surf for as long as possible. On a really hot wave, sometimes you go unfortunately too far and this results in not being able to get out again because all the following waves are breaking directly in front of you.

An important psychological factor is how easy or how difficult you find it to get out to the line-up. Despite excellent duck-diving techniques, it can be frustrating and intimidating when you have to battle for hours to get out at all. Thus a good knowledge of the local conditions is important.

You have to be able to take advantage of currents to make your way out easier and save energy. Let's have a look at a typical big-wave-day on a beachbreak. Some way out to sea the waves are breaking on a sandbank. The white water rolls all the way to the beach. If, during your surf check, you spot an area near the outside sandbank where hardly any waves are breaking – a sort of passage – then of course you know where you want to paddle out. Sounds simple, but the problem is that you have to do about 20 duck-dives through the white water in order to reach this passage. With a current running sideways at the same time, you lose a few metres every time you duck-dive. If you try paddling directly towards the passage it is more than likely that you will never reach it because you will be driven off-course by the current. Therefore

Hawaiian power – big waves are sometimes as broad as they are high. (Photo by Chiemsee, photographer: Erik Aeder)

calculate the current and enter the water 100 or so metres upstream. This problem does not exist at most reefs and point breaks. The waves break only in one area. Around the reef the water is deeper and hardly any waves break here. There is often a current which makes the paddling out much easier. At point breaks, where waves break along a headland, occasionally you can simply enter the water on the other side of the headland. This way you actually paddle into the line-up from behind. Another – somewhat risky – possibility is to jump off the rocks at the tip of the headland directly behind the breakline. Doing this gets you out into big waves, almost with your hair still dry so to speak. On one hand this is simple and saves energy. On the other, for the inexperienced surfer or beginner, the natural barrier of the white water, mentioned earlier, is no longer there so that he gets out into waves that may be too big for his degree of skill.

Currents around reefs and entering the water by jumping off the rocks bear another danger. The entry and exit points in and out of the water are often in different places. This means that beforehand you must take a good look at where and how other surfers are leaving the water. Very often the beach is dotted with outcrops of rocks and reefs, and there are only a few spots where you can get out. This is particularly critical in big waves. For example, in Uluwatu (Bali, Indonesia) the entry and exit point is through a cave. Paddling out of the cave is not a problem, but with big waves and a strong current, finding your way back into the cave demands a certain amount of skill and courage. So first of all watch and learn from the others.

Currents in big waves can be extremely strong. One spot we surfed in Tahitii, where 4 to 5-footers were good fun, turned out to be totally different and intimidating at 6 to 8-foot. There was so much water flowing between the reef that you had to constantly keep paddling not to get sucked out to sea. Of course this was very tiring and we soon decided we had had enough. If the current is also running towards a harbour wall, rocks, dry reef or something similar it can get dangerous. You must leave the water before you get too exhausted. If you do not feel 100% – maybe a hangover from the night before – you should realise what to expect in the water and what you will be capable of.

Now let's get down to actually surfing big waves. Basically it is almost simpler than surfing small waves. You have a little more time for everything. Above all, this is because there is simply more waves to surf on. You can really get the feeling of gliding. The drop lasts longer; the same applies for the bottom turn or the cutback. A larger surfboard will allow you to catch the wave early. You can possibly correct your stance and keep on riding in a firm position. A low stance with bent knees is important to be able to absorb any unevenness on the surface of the wave.

Cutback on a mountain of a wave
(Photo: Joli)

When surfing take care that all your movements are done smoother and with more flow than in small waves. When you are driving at top speed on the freeway you should not be making radical movements with the steering wheel. Big waves are somehow the freeway of the waves (we have just made that up).

Top turns are no longer done right on the top of the wave, and generally the manoeuvres are a little less radical. The waves are radical enough in themselves. Otherwise you do everything else as normal. You see there is very little that is different. Just how well you can ride big waves depends largely on what is going on in your head. A little bit of angst and adrenaline is OK, but you must never panic because you will eventually make a dangerous mistake. This already begins with the take-off. At all costs do not hesitate. In big waves the worst type of wipe-out occurs when you hesitate and then you come crashing down together with the lip of the wave. If your drop is successful for the first half and you "only" wipe-out at the base of the wave then it is not half as bad. So, as with hollow waves, when you have decided to go for a wave, give everything to catch it. But just as in small waves, It is important to give the two extra strokes even if you think you have caught the wave. Try to remain relaxed in the water even if the waves are awesome. You can work on this as you continually expand your ability and limitations. If you are still a little afraid in 5-foot waves, you should soon think about having a go at your first session in 6 to 8-footers. You do not necessarily have to take a wave. Keep yourself near one of the channels and watch out particularly for big sets. Just getting used to and dealing with these kind of conditions will make your next session in 5-footers that much easier. Best of all make your first attempts at big waves in the company of people who are more experienced or better surfers than you are. They can give you tips where to sit and wait for waves and above all they will make the whole atmosphere a bit more relaxed. If you are surprised by a set and a huge foam wall is coming at you, your instinct demands that you throw away your board and dive underneath the wave. In big waves this can be disastrous. If you do not duck-dive properly, and the wave is powerful enough, it will rip your leash off as if it were nothing. The result is that you will be drifting around in huge surf without your surfboard. On top of this a powerful wave will may even break your beloved board in half like a matchstick. Apart from the danger that your louse board (attached to your foot or not) will present to all the others in the water, you should think carefully about whether you want to go through all of this if you do not duck-dive. Even if you are thoroughly bashed about, you will still have your surfboard after a duck-dive, and in big waves this can be vital. There are, however, situations when a duck-dive is impossible. This happens mostly when the wave breaks immediately in front of or over you. All you can do is to get off the board, and, before the wave hits you, give the board a push so that it moves away parallel to the wave e.g., parallel to the beach. This reduces the risk of breaking it, since logically it is easier to break a matchstick (your surfboard) sideways rather than lengthways. Again, you should bail out in an emergency only.

Now for a few important "psycho tips" that will perhaps sound a bit ridiculous or stupid, but which are very effective. After a while you will of course develop your own motivation tricks.

- Before going into the water say to yourself, "Unreal-big waves at last!" and not "Oh my god, aren't they huge!"
- If the wave holds you underwater for long, just think you are a cork in the water. Sometime or the other you will surface back up again. Keeping your eyes open and counting helps you to avoid panicking.
- Fire yourself up with other surfers to go for the waves. Just as you are about to hesitate on the take-off a loud shout from your friends of "Go, go, go, goooo!" works wonders.

Before you go surfing, listen to the music that motivates you the most. There is nothing worse than having a poor song drumming in your mind. As motivation in big waves we always use music a little on the harder side that fits the scene. Pantera's "Vulgar Display of Power" has served us well. Other tunes like Tom Petty's, "Free Falling" did not work as well for some reason. But It is not all hard music. We have had some good sessions with "No, you're never gonna get it" by En Vogue spinning in our ears. Each to his own though. We are sure you will soon find the right tune.

3.3   Manoeuvres for the Advanced

Actually we have already described the most important manoeuvre – the tube. But you are right, if you spend all your time in the tube, you will never get a real sun tan. So here are a few more tips for radical manoeuvres.

It does not get much more radical – the snap!
(Photo: O'Neill, photographer: Bill Morris)

We are not going to tell you in which direction and when you have to turn your shoulder, or at what angle you have to stretch your arm out. You will find this out for yourself. But, there are a few things that, if you keep them in your head when you are out surfing the next time, will be quite useful.

Off-the-lip

*T*he off-the-lip turn is a great manoeuvre to learn. Simply because you will find it good fun from the beginning and you will be able to do it even more radically as your skills improve. It is not difficult to learn. In its various different versions you will hear the off-the-lip also being called "re-entry" ('reo' for short) and "off-the-top" amongst others. It is all about one thing: doing a top-turn, not only when you are at the top of the wave, but also up as far as where the lip begins to break and then doing a turn on or with the lip and thereby building up more speed. The difficulty is that the very thing on top of which you want to turn, is coming towards you. Once again It is a question of timing. If you are too far away from the curl, the turn will be, firstly very difficult, and secondly, there will be no lip there for your off-the-lip turn. This means that you really have to turn where the wave begins to break. The key to a successful off-the-lip is the angle at which you approach the lip.

Backhand off-the-lip; board in the vertical position with lots of leg pressure (Photo: Joli)

The more vertical you approach the lip, the easier the actual turn, but the more radical the manoeuvre will be. This means that you will be practically going directly upwards. The aim is that the lip hits the bottom of the board, and not the side or your feet. After your bottom turn, you are not heading towards the safety of the shoulder, but vertically upwards to the lip. The later you meet the lip as it comes down, the more vertical your board will lie on the wave in the moment of the turn. If you do not have sufficient power in your legs or your timing is wrong, it can happen that the lip will knock your board into your face. Take care! The moment that you turn on the lip is almost like hitting it, hence the expression "to hit the lip". Well, you know, sometimes it can also hit back.

Floater

*T*his manoeuvre has not been around for a long. We can remember exactly when we were in France sometime or the other and were watching a surfer, who somehow was surfing better than anything we had seen there before. He was not only faster than all the rest, he simply surfed over the white water when a wave closed down in front of him and continued his ride on the unbroken part of the wave – just like that. "Hey this guy just did an ... um ... err ... what-shall-we-call-it ... a floater!" The surfer was Tom Curren who was the dominating surfer in the eighties, and still today is seen by some as one of the best surfers of all times.

The aim of the floater is to get past the section of the wave that is breaking in front of you, and pick up your surfing line again beyond it. Before some surfer invented the floater (it was not Tom Curren), once a section broke in front of you the ride was over. So it is really a very practical manoeuvre. Again the deciding factor (for any radical manoeuvre) is speed, vitesse, tempo. If you do not have enough speed it will not work. So you build up your speed by trimming up and down the face, because you realise that the section in front of you is about to close down. At the moment the wave breaks, you ride onto and over the foam. You are now actually going against the energy of the wave. If you do not have enough speed the wave will simply throw you off the board. But, how do you get onto the foam? At the moment you reach the white water you must unweight your board. Just imagine that you have footstraps on your board and you want to jump up with your board. Now adjust the motion to the fact that you do not have footstraps. Of course you do not want to jump right up otherwise your board will logically be left behind.

Nevertheless you have to really take the weight off both of your feet. The foam underneath will press the board up and ensure that you do not lose it. Additionally you can somewhat raise your arms to assist the unweighting action. Once again you must make sure that the bottom of the board hits the breaking part of the wave. Many make the mistake of pressing the rail into the foam. Try to raise the front of your board up just before you meet the foam so that the wave only comes into contact with the underside of the board and glides along it.

By the way, river surfing also works on this principle. You are not flushed away by the stream of the river because it is passing underneath the bottom of the board – endless floater so to speak.

The difficulty with the floater is that, firstly, going against the impetus of the wave slows you down, which makes keeping your balance difficult, and secondly you have problems controlling your board because the fins have no grip in the foam.

The landing is also not without its problems. Often the transition from the foam to the unbroken part of the wave is somewhat rough. You must keep your knees bent and absorb the impact of the transition as you leave the foam. It is quite possible you will do a little free fall, which is a good point to move on to the next section.

Floater Rob Machado (Photos by Chiemsee, photographer: Erik Aeder)

Aerial

Aerials come from skateboarding. This is when the skateboarder jumps about 2 metres up out of a half-pipe and lands back down in it again. Since many skateboarders are also surfers, it was only a question of time before the first ones would be jumping out of the waves and landing back on them again. One of the first to do this was the South African Martin Potter. In the meantime an aerial with a built-in 180° or 360° spin belongs to the standard repertoire of each serious new schooler. Aerials are great fun and look spectacular but actually have no real purpose (like for instance the floater has). But since most useless things often provide the best fun, here are a few tips. Practice your first aerials like a skateboard "ollie hop". This means jumping as you go along by doing a sort of flicking movement with the feet (there's really no other way to describe it), lifting your board up at the same time. The flicking movement is done by pushing down your rear and your front foot quickly one after the other starting with the rear. You can use little chops on the wave as launch pads to make things easier.

The other way of doing an aerial is to start doing an off-the-lip without actually turning on impact with the lip. Instead you just shoot off over the lip. Once again speed is the key for success. Being able to land after an aerial is usually more by accident than design, but there are some people who regularly pull it off. It is particularly critical that you do not lose contact with the board while you are in the air. If your board lands just in front of you and you try to land on it, this will be the end of your board. This is why you must try to grab the board in flight with one hand just like in skateboarding. Even if you never manage to successfully complete an aerial, just trying is fun enough. So – get air!

Get air! (Photo: O'Neill, photographer: Bill Morris)

The Round House Cutback

ou already know about the cutback from the section for beginners. If you want to give it a little extra, first of all put more pressure on the inside rail and lean further into the turn, secondly, do a figure of eight. Do a cutback in the direction of the breaking wave – and now comes the icing on the cake – you surf back to the breaking lip (actually going against the breaking direction of the wave) and on the lip you do – yes, just what you thought – an off-the-lip or re-entry, only this time it is called a "rebound". Try to think of it like this: first the cutback then an off-the-lip on the approaching wave. If you can get this into one flowing sequence it looks very fluid and radical.

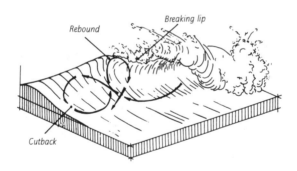

Rebound *Breaking lip*

Cutback

1 x 8 =the round house cutback (Drawing: Stefan "Muli" Müller)

The Snap and/or Tail-slide

"snap" or "tail-slide" is done almost out on the shoulder (just under or on the edge of the lip). The difference to a normal top-turn is that this manoeuvre is a much more radical and powerful change of direction. You really have to apply a lot of pressure with your rear leg and foot which then often creates a fountain of water high up over the edge of the wave. This is also called "to throw some spray". The key is the amount of power placed on the rear leg. Just have a look at the legs of Tom Carroll, and then you will know why he is the only one who does a snap under the lip in a 10 to 12-foot pipeline. Because of the high pressure on the tail of the board, this will easily break away in a snap, and then you are doing a tail-slide. To be able to control this slide is difficult and requires a very radical manoeuvre. It is especially easy to do a tail-slide if you do the snap high enough up on the wave that the fins break free beyond the curl, and are practically, for a short time, free in the air letting the board slide. Here you need balance. The further up the wave you do the snap, the easier it is to push your board through the turn. On the other hand you risk being thrown off the surfboard by the lip. If you do not want to be all that radical, you can do the tail-slide on the shoulder of the wave by pushing the tail round hard and at the same time putting some weight on the forward foot. This way the tail lifts slightly out of the water, the fins have less grip, and the turning movement will be easier – the board slides quicker so to speak.

Throwing spray! (Photo: Fanatic)

Tail-slides are often a controversially discussed manoeuvre. Some surfers are of the opinion that they are a useless gimmick compared to a turn where you fully bury your rail. Although, full power turns, from rail to rail, are what performance surfing is all about, tail-slides are great fun and there is no reason why you should not try one. To be able to have the best of both worlds is probably the ideal way, and this is why six times world champion Kelly Slater is the dominating surfer of this decade.

The 360°-turn

Of course what we are talking about here is turning through 360° i.e., all the way round in one movement. This is actually a trick, which has regained popularity over the last few years among the new surfing generation (also called "The New School"), with surfers as Kelly Slater, Rob Machado, Tim Curren and others.

First of all you start a forehand turn up the wave. The tip of your board goes (just like the off-the-lip) straight up the wave only this time you go even further than straight. This means that the tip of the board will be at 11 o'clock for goofys and at 1 o'clock for regulars (both frontside), with the curl being at 12 o'clock. Now the lip or the foam presses against the rail now closest to the lip and this pushes you round the roughly remaining 170° of the turn. The critical thing is to go up the wave face "a little more than straight". The remainder is done by the wave almost on its own. Some really hot surfers use the moment when the tail is pointing down to the bottom of the wave to put some weight on to the front foot – the nose – so that they manage to surf backwards for a short time. In the "Surfers Dictionary" you will find this under "reverse".

3.4 General Tips for the Advanced

- Reefs are only for the advanced. Although points and sandbanks also offer some challenging waves, they usually provide a good ride for everyone.

- Paddle hard in big or hollow waves. Always put in a couple of extra strokes, even when you think you have caught the wave. do not be tempted to try a late take-off.

- Do not hesitate in large or hollow waves.

- Do not panic underwater. This uses up important energy.

- Learn to control your fears. Psycho tricks can help.

- Do not take the first wave in a set. If you try to and then end up not catching it, all the following waves will break on your head.

- Take a good long look at the surfing spot: currents, rocks, shallows, channels, the take-off area, boomer-sets etc.

- Do not panic if your leash breaks. Never try to swim against the current. Always swim back in with the white water.

- Make use of lulls (pauses between sets) to get out to the line-up.

- Always duck-diving.

- The secret for all manoeuvres is speed.

- Getting tubed is the ultimate thrill. Keep your eyes open in the tube and put pressure on your inside-rail.

- Get out of the water while you still have the strength.

- Obey the rules of surfing. The surfer on the inside always has the right of way.

- **"Do not drop-in!" and "Respect the locals!"**

- **But our most important tip is: "Get out there and have fun!"**

Worth a trip! (Photo: Menges/Diel)

IV. WAVES AROUND THE WORLD

surfer must sooner or later go out and search for the perfect wave. Even if you have a surfspot right on your doorstep, you will one day travel to another country to surf unknown waves. Believe us – there are spots out there, where on certain days, everything simply comes together and the waves can only be described in one word – perfect. To find these places, above all you need two things, time and money. But since time is money as one says, you will have saved half of the problem already.

Of course, we cannot help you to find the necessary small change for your surfing trip. However, we can help you with saving time on the spot. Where is the surf? How do I get there, and when is the wave season? We have gathered together quite a bit of useful information from our own travels over the years.

Of course, we have not checked out every possible surfspot in the world and therefore we concentrate on those places where we have surfed ourselves. If you are interested to hear about where, when and how, join us on this little surftrip around the world.

1   Tips for a Surfari

Where to go

he factors time and money are the two variables that decide where to go. Surfers are well-known for doing without luxury resorts in exchange for good surf. Who wants a hotel with a pool when 6-foot barrels are breaking on the doorstep? Who wants a breakfast buffet when there is fresh fruit on every street corner? Naturally no-one is against a bit of comfort, but you should really think twice whether you want to invest in a better hotel or in more miles on your air ticket. Our experience is that usually getting there is the most expensive part of the trip. Eating and drinking at home also costs something. If you can manage to keep your expenses for accommodation and travel on the ground (hire car etc.,) to a minimum, you can last with little money for a relatively long time (more waves!). The secret is: cheap flights, cheap accommodation and cheap transport.

Time is the other factor that will limit your moves. The shorter the time available, the less time you will want to spend sitting in a car or plane to get there and back. For a one-week's trip, a 3-hour flight is more suitable than a 20-hour flight to somewhere like Australia. On top of that there is also the jet lag. Many Australia-travellers need a full week to get over the jet lag. It was quite funny when, on our trip through the South Pacific we crossed the International Date Line. We took off on the 9th of June and landed on the 8th of June. We gained a day.

If you have a lot of time It is worthwhile to go looking for 'lonely' waves in exotic places. If time is short, preferably stick to the beaten track where you do not have to go searching for waves and where you know the conditions. A further alternative is to book into a surf camp where, besides transport and accommodation, local knowledge of the area is all-inclusive and provided by the organisers. Surf camps can be found in various places; in Europe, Australia, California and also Indonesia and the South Pacific. More about this later.

Besides having enough time, the wave season in the chosen surfing destination is also a factor. Somewhere in the world there is always someone surfing. The film, "The Endless Summer", illustrates this in a way that has sent thousands of surfers around the world in search for waves. A bit of a frustrating image when you are sitting at home saving for your next surfing trip. In the Northern hemisphere the summer lasts from June to September. In the Southern hemisphere It is exactly the opposite. When It is summer in the Northern hemisphere, It is winter in the southern part, and when the north is shivering in winter (November to February), the south is basking in summer sunshine. But there are places, like Hawaii for instance, where it never gets really cold and the water is always warm, and you can surf all year round (on different coasts though). In several countries there are not four seasons but only the difference between the wet and the dry season. But you should be able to get this sort of information from your travel agent. What he will most likely not be able to answer, is when the waves will be breaking in the different places. The following table will give you a few clues as to where the tubes are hiding at different times of year (the details are based on the Northern hemisphere seasons).

Europe (France, Spain, Portugal)	All year round, best at end of summer In summer unsettled, in winter cold
Hawaii	November to April Medium to monster-sized waves
Indonesia (Bali)	May to August Dry season on the west coast (Uluwatu) December to March Monsoon season (Nusa Dua)
Australia	Winter East Coast (Queensland, New South Wales) Summer South and West Coast
South Pacific (Fiji, Tahiti etc.)	May to August
Mexico	Winter North Baja Summer South Baja and Mainland
Costa Rica	All year round Winter, dry season, Caribbean side Summer, wet season, Pacific side
California	All year round In winter big waves but very cold water

If you have made your selection, there are a number of ways to learn more about the land of your dreams. Here are a few for you to choose from:

Get a copy of the "Surf Report". Surf Report publishes monthly detailed information about different surfing destinations. The editions that have been published up to date are always listed in the American "Surfer" magazine. Check the number of the edition with your target country and request the information by fax. Each edition costs about $US 6.50, and can be ordered under the fax number USA/949/49 67 849.

Most of the surfing magazines in Australia or the USA will answer readers letters about surfing places. Magazines such as "Surfer" and "Surfing" in the USA and "Tracks" in Australia are examples.

There are some specialised surfing travel agencies around and you can find out about them in surf magazines or on the Internet. One we have dealt with is the Surf Travel Company (STC) in Australia, which will give you tips by fax over the best seasons in the various surf spots. Naturally they want you to book a trip with them. STC offers package deals, specially tailored for the particular needs of surfers, and these trips are well-recommended. They are experts for Indonesia and the South Pacific. Simply fax them on +61/2/95 27 45 22 and find out what is on offer. A little tip: if you get a good priced offer from another travel agency, try STC as they will often try to beat the price. The STC web page is also a good source of information on various exotic surf locations (www.surftravel.com.au)

You could, however, also invest a little more time and read this book to the end.

What to bring

Packing for a trip. Isn't that a great feeling? You will know for yourself what clothing to take with you – or simply ask your mom. But, what surfing equipment do you need? As a basic principle – as much as necessary and as little as possible. Once you have dragged your giant travel bag, plus several surfboards, through a steaming hot exotic airport, you will swear to pack only half next time.

Boards

We always take two boards with us on our travels. A shortboard about 6.5 feet long for waves up to 5 feet, and a gun about 7 feet long for the larger waves. We really recommend boards with removable fins for the journey.

Be sure to check the extra charge the airline will make for carrying your boards as a second piece of luggage. Some make no charge, others will charge so much that you could buy a new board at your destination for the same money.

If you want to, or are only able to take one board with you, it should be an all-round board that should rather be a little longer than normal. You will, of course, need a little more power to push the board around in small waves, which you will soon get used to, but for all that you will be more confident in larger waves. You do not have to hold back when you finally find the perfect 6-foot waves you travelled for.

Board Bag

You must always look after and protect your beloved surfboard. Surfboards get easily damaged. On top of this, airport personnel usually do not handle your luggage with the greatest of care. In some languages it seems that the sticker "Fragile" means something along the lines of: "This surfboard is especially suitable for throwing the heaviest and hardest piece of luggage on top of it." This is why a board bag is an absolute must. Ideal is a bag that will take two boards. If the airline accepts a second piece of luggage without charging extra, you can pass off your second board in one stroke with your double board bag. The board bag should be one with robust exterior material and a reliable solid zip, which you can unzip hundreds of times, despite all the sand and saltwater getting in the works. A board bag may also double as a sleeping bag or mattress for nights under the stars in the open.

Wax or Grip Deck?

For travelling, full decks are quite practical. To start with your bag will not smell of coconut/strawberry aromatised wax, and it could be that (this is the more important reason) you will not necessarily be able to buy wax everywhere you go.

The disadvantage with grip decks is the fact that you can easily get a rash if you surf only in shorts. Wearing a wetshirt can eliminate this problem. If you do not necessarily have to prove that you have had a fantastic trip by showing off a suntan, wearing a wetshirt when in the water is better for your skin. Whether there is a hole in the ozone layer or not, too much sun is basically damaging to the skin. A suitably factor-graded, water repellant suntan cream and a zinc sun blocker should not be missing from your list.

Wetsuit

When it comes to the wetsuit you have to know what the water temperature is at your destination. Even if the water is warm, like for instance in Bali, wearing a vest or something similar can protect you from cuts on a reef. Countries where you must, at all costs, take a wetsuit with long legs and arms are Europe (Spain, France, Great Britain etc.), California, Australia and New Zealand during their winter, and South Africa. In addition take one or two wetshirts for the sun and as protection against getting a rash from the rubbing of your wetsuit. Surf boots are also a must for all surfing destinations where there are coral reefs or sea urchins. If you do not intend to be scared of 6-foot top-to-bottom waves, we recommend you also to take a helmet.

Other Things

Sooner or later, It is guaranteed that your surfboard will get a ding. Most little cracks can be repaired by yourself with some resin and catalyst. There are especially made-up repair kits for travelling in which you will find everything you need to do a small repair job. Products such as

"Solarez" (resin out of the tube) have proved to be very practical. In this case the resin requires no catalyst, because It is already contained in the product. Ultraviolet rays cause a chemical reaction and the resin hardens in seconds. Make sure to fix your board in the shade. As soon as the mixture is in sunlight the magic begins to work. The practical part about it is that you will not get the mixing proportions wrong and all you have to carry around is a little tube of resin and some sandpaper – just in case you need it.

Travel Guides

Besides a special surfing guide for each country, that will help you to find the best waves, you should also get your hands on a general tourist guidebook with information about currency, health care and services, local customs and habits, accommodation, consulates etc. On our trips the guides from "Lonely Planet" proved to be very useful everywhere we went, especially the tips concerning value for money accommodation and food.

There are many guidebooks about. However you should check whether you have the same understanding of the words "cheap" or "interesting" as the author of the book.

Health

At all costs you need to take a small medical kit with you. Peroxide for disinfecting, medicine for diarrhoea and band aids are all essential contents.

In many exotic countries there is still a threat of malaria (e.g., in Nias, Indonesia). The danger zones change as rapidly as the most efficient remedies do. An Institute for Tropical Medicine, doctors specialising in tropical medicine, health authorities and some airlines can all give you information regarding the necessary prophylactic measures. However, now close your bag, get the surfboards on the roof rack and let's get moving to the airport. Let's go surfing!

2   Europe

*T*here is something funny about Europe. All the European surfers want to go to Australia or America, while all the Australians or Americans particularly want to go to Europe to surf. And they are right! In Europe you can find really good waves all the year round. The waves are often underrated. The beach breaks in Hossegor, the tubes in Mundacca, the reefs in Portugal and on the Canary Islands are all world-class. There is not much point in trying, in this chapter, to list or describe all the good European spots, because others have already done this in an excellent way. The "Stormrider Guide" (available in most surf shops in Europe) describes almost every spot in Europe. It tells you when and where the waves are breaking – if you plan to surf in Europe this guidebook is an absolute 'must-have'. We would like, nevertheless, to tell you about a few of our own experiences to help you on your way.

France

Although we have surfed some good waves in Nice, we want to restrict ourselves here to the Atlantic coast south of Bordeaux. There are lots of reports and also photos of waves in the Mediterranean – but between you and me, these are only exceptions. In complete contrast, the Atlantic coast is a totally different thing. Of course there are periods, sometimes lasting more than a week, when the Atlantic pretty much resembles the Mediterranean. You will find waves on the Atlantic coast all year round. However, only the real hard core surfers go out here in winter because the water is really very cold. The best time for waves is late summer to autumn. Since this fact is, meanwhile, well-known round the world, several professional surf contests are held here during this season. That means that from August onwards there is a lot going on in and out of the water at the popular spots, and this sometimes creates a bit of an aggressive attitude in the water. The French Atlantic coast, however, has one disadvantage, which funnily enough turns into an advantage when there are too many people in the water. The disadvantage is that the coast is basically a single, long, straight stretch of beach. This means that when the wind is blowing hard from the north, it practically blows out the whole coast, since there are no headlands or bays to protect the waves from the wind. As a result, conditions along the coast on any one day are the same all along it. For instance, if It is bad here, then 50 km further on, it will hardly be any better. The big advantage, however, is that if you are at a spot with 50 other people and the surf is pumping, it is very probable that you will find the same good conditions on some other beach also. Although the conditions are often very similar, there are differences in the quality of the waves. Dependent on the sandbanks, on which the waves break, there can be enormous differences. A spot where the waves broke perfectly in one year may produce only closed out-waves the next year when the sandbanks have changed. This leads to everybody having his own secret spot to go to with a few friends for a quiet session. This is the really fascinating part about France. Although so many surfers go there year after year, you can always find your own secret spot behind Dune No 12 again. A further considerable influence on the quality of waves are the tides. The differences between low and high tide can be extreme. The waves that break during low tide will often be considerably different to the waves at high tide. Some experience is required to understand all these numerous factors and make use of them. You will soon know when and where the waves are breaking. Two friends, who mastered this many years ago, are Uli and Martin from the surf school "Wave Tours". They are both Germans, but have been running surf camps in France for several years. They offer ideal surf courses for both beginners and the advanced in a relaxed and comfortable camping atmosphere. The course includes accommodation in a top camping site, equipment (including board and wetsuit), transportation to the various surf spots and coaching as well as many other good fun things. The guys from "Wave Tours" have a lot of experience with landlubbers, some of whom one would have really considered to be absolute hopeless. If you want to make your first attempts a lot easier, book a course with Uli and Martin to start with. Advanced surfers can of course also learn a thing or two from them. You can reach them by phone on +49 6151-4 57 27. We can recommend the "Wave Tours" boys, not only because of the way they teach, but simply because you will also have a good time with them and other surfers.

The Atlantic coast is, as we have already said, basically one single stretch of surfing beach that starts just above Bordeaux and runs down to St Jean de Luz near the Spanish border. Here are a few of the best spots.

Lacanau Ocean

The water in summer is still relatively a little fresh here. In the last few years tourism has rather taken the upper hand in the town itself as far as we are concerned. Accordingly, there is quite a lot of activity in the water. However, to the north and south of the town there are a number of lonely beaches with good waves. In the south, the road (an old tank track) behind the dunes is sometimes blocked off. If you park your car, and walk a few metres, you will be able to find a beach almost all to yourself. And for those who do not know yet - you will find out soon enough though - nude sunbathing and swimming is very much the fashion away from the main beaches in France.

Hossegor/ Seignosse

Here you will find probably the most powerful beach breaks on the whole of the Atlantic. Given the right conditions you will have all the tubes you can handle.

The main surf spot in Hossegor actually belongs to the village of Seignosse, and is called les Estagnots. If you are going towards Hossegor, drive in the direction of the sea, and just before you get to the beach go on the road behind the dunes northwards towards Seignosse. As you pass the town signpost the road goes up to the left to Plage des Estagnots or Cote Sauvage (wild coast). You will eventually come to the legendary parking place that, in the high season, looks more like a campsite with surfers from all over the world. On the beach itself there are three main peaks. Using the lifeguards' hut on the dune as 12 o'clock there is a wave that breaks directly in a line with this hut. A second wave breaks at 2 o'clock, and a third at 11 o'clock. Surf the one that is least crowded. For whatever reason, surfers suffer from the 'sheep syndrome', because whenever a couple of surfers are sitting in the water, suddenly there is the next one and so on until there is a 'herd' of them. do not play this game! Just try out the uncrowded wave on the next sandbank. Still, if you are a beginner it is essential here for you to have someone keeping an eye open for you. Above all, if you are together with friends, do not think about herding in another five more sheep.

Oh là là! Eric in France (Photo: Menges/Diel)

In Hossegor if you follow the signpost to "Front de Mer", you will come to the notorious Rock Food – the favourite surfers hangout with parties, videos etc. When the swell is really big and everything else is closed out, directly in front of Rock Food there is an excellent wave. Further to the south of Hossegor, in the town of Capbreton is la Piste, easy to recognise because of the World War II German bunkers that line the beach. This is another quality beach break with numerous peaks.

Biarritz

Biarritz is the surfing capital of France. Plenty of surf shops and many good surf spots is its trademark. To the north of Biarritz, in the direction of Bayonne, lies Chambre d'amour. In the shadows of a tall cliff the beach has been artificially divided up into a number of little beaches. The rocky pier deposits have created a particularly interesting sandbank formation with a good beach break. The locals in Biarritz can sometimes be a little oversensitive so they must be handled with care. Show respect but do not let them pick on you. North of Chambre d'amour the River Adour flows into the sea. A long stone pier has been built on the south side of the river mouth. Some time ago, one of the best waves in Europe broke on the north side of the pier – La Barre. Today the waves here have lost most of their quality but they are often your last hope if the wind is blowing too strongly from the south, as the pier offers protection from it. It is a different story on the south side of the pier. On the Plage des Cavaliers, the waves are often some of the best in the whole Biarritz area since the stone pier offers good protection from the prevailing north wind. Additionally, next to the pier there is a current running out to sea, which the surfers can use as a sort of conveyor belt to get out into the line-up.

In Biarritz, the main beach itself, la Grand Plage, is relatively well-protected from southerly and northerly winds. However, aggressive high spirited and a high degree of water pollution often spoil the fun here. The highlight here was a dead rat that floated past us in the water.

To the south of Biarritz, towards the Spanish border there are some reefs, which for France is extremely unusual. These reefs need a strong swell to function properly. Lafitenia has a powerful right-hander, and at Guethary a big perfect peak breaks left and right. In the town of the same name you drive in the direction of Cenitz or the harbour. The wave breaks about 200 m out from the beach. Beyond Guethary keep an eye open for the signpost "Acotz" to get to Lafitenia. The road leads up to a large parking place. From here you have to walk down a steep road about 100 m to the beach. The wave breaks to your right. Looking around and searching is all part of the game, particularly as there are many more spots in this area which you may well stumble upon.

Spain

Coming from Biarritz you drive directly into the legendary Basque country. The Basques are a little reserved when it comes to dealing with tourists and sometimes they can even be somewhat arrogant. However, a friendly smile often breaks the ice.

San Sebastian has an old part of the town that offers an exiting night-life. The typical tapas-bars are our favourites. On the weekend you think that you are at a festival, but this is normal here. If you take the motorway towards Bilbao you are well on the road to Mundacca and the amazing waves there. At Amorebieta turn off in the direction of Guernica, and then towards Bermeo until, just before you get to Bermeo, you land up in the town of Mundacca. The waves break in the river mouth directly behind the unmistakable landmark of the village church. Without doubt, Mundacca is the best and longest left wave in Europe and surely it is one of the best in the world. Tubes, tubes, tubes. Although the waves break on a sandy bottom, they are very powerful. Multiple tubes on one single wave are quite common. But you have to be quick. The waves are so long and fast that, after continually pumping, your legs will beg for mercy. We arrived in Mundacca at high tide and immediately thought our journey had been a waste of time because nothing was breaking. As the tide began to go out, the picture changed from one minute to the next, and we could not get into our wetsuits fast enough. The way out to the line-up goes through the little fishing harbour. You paddle through the absolutely calm waters of the harbour.

As soon as you leave the harbour waters, you are off. A strong current running along the harbour wall pulls you straight out into the middle of the line-up. Mundacca has to be handled with caution during a large swell, because the place has a few surprises in store.

Mundacca – what a set up (watch for the current in front of the harbour wall on the very left in the picture) (Photo: Joli)

The waves break right in the entrance of a river and they depend very much on the tide. When the tide goes out all the water flows out to sea, and in seconds you will be pulled out quite a distance and spend the rest of the time paddling back to get to the line-up. Paddling for the wave, you will also be fighting against the current, resulting in a somewhat late, steep and difficult take-off. As the tide comes in this little game runs the other way round. Water is pressed into the river mouth. If you see a big set coming in, and you want to paddle towards it, you will find you are hardly moving because of the current. From 6-footers upward it gets a little hairy. After a successful ride the current will make the return to the line-up difficult.

However, you can use the water running out to sea along the harbour wall regardless of high or low tide. This same current is used to get back into the harbour waters. You ride a wave as far as it goes up the river and then paddle back into the current along the harbour wall, as mentioned already. You must keep a little to the left whilst in the current, and just before the harbour entrance you must paddle hard to get out of the current. If you do not keep far enough to the left, you will not make it, and you will have to go round again.

The Mundacca locals are a special breed. You could almost call them the matadors of the surf. Being fearless and relatively aggressive, sometimes they do not always have everything under control. Act friendly and let them have their waves. Arguing is useless. Sometime or other a wave, with your name on it, will come along. If you treat the locals with respect they will leave the odd wave for you. A single wave in Mundacca is sufficient enough to freeze a grin on your face for a long time.

Around Mundacca, as well as around the region of Zarautz, there are numerous other spots that are worth the trip. "Hasta la vista, baby!"

Portugal

The Portuguese Atlantic coast is the ideal spot to get away from the surfing hordes in France. The journey there by car takes a lot of time, but one has to accept this in order to find some uncrowded waves. An alternative is to fly to Lisbon and hire a car there. Some of the surf spots are in the immediate vicinity of the town. Portugal is very reasonable and good value, and the people are very friendly.

The water is super-cold, even in summer. Bring a full suit. Interestingly the temperature of the water in winter does not drop all that much. Thus, surfing in the colder seasons is still a possibility. The best time of year is therefore from September onwards. For your evening entertainment we recommend a visit to the local cinema. The films are in English (with Portuguese sub-titles) and entry costs around US $2.

Although you can surf along the whole of the Atlantic coast, the surfing scene is concentrated around the areas of Ericeira and Peniche. Ericeira is well-known for its reefs (infested with sea urchins), which produce fantastic waves. Make a note of the name "Coxos". On the Baleal peninsula near the town of Peniche you will always find a wave with an offshore wind, irrespective where the wind is coming from because you can surf on both sides of the peninsula. On one side there is a beach break, and on the other a reef with lots of sweet little sea urchins. Nevertheless It is a great area. Nearby is also the spot 'Supertubes' – the name says it all.

The Canaries

Up until now we have only surfed on the island of Fuerteventura. However, all the islands here offer good surfing. Particularly worth mentioning is La Santa on Lanzarote. The Canary Islands is the Hawaii of Europe. Powerful waves in warm temperatures in the middle of winter. The water is not cold, but in winter your wetsuit should have long legs and at least short sleeves.

Fuerteventura

Although practically the whole year round waves break on all sides of the island, the warm temperatures in winter are the special attraction. During this time of the year the north shore comes alive. There is a good reef break after the other.

When in Fuerteventura your first call should therefore be Sigi Opitz. He has lived on Fuerteventura for many years and knows all the spots like the back of his hand. Together with his girlfriend, Maria, he runs a really cool surf camp in Corralejo called "Ineika Funcenter". Whether you are a beginner in the surf school with Bernhard the Swiss surf legend, or an advanced surfer doing a guided tour with Sigi himself, the name Funcenter justifiably means exactly that. On top of that, the price is

Sigi at work in his backyard off the Corralejo harbour (Photo: Ineika)

SURFING

136

extremely fair. The atmosphere at the Ineika is easygoing and relaxing. A surf course in Ineika is therefore bound to be a success, because having fun is the top priority. The quality waves on Fuerteventura do the rest. We keep coming back and always have a great time at the Ineika, and we are sure you will experience the same.

You can contact Sigi on +34/928/535744 (phone & fax). By the way, the airport transfer charge is included in the price. Sigi Opitz is the one who knows where the tubes are and believe us he knows how to pull in.

3.   USA and Hawaii

The United States is one of the surfing Meccas of the world. This is where one can surf on 8,000 km of beaches on the west and east coast of the mainland, including Alaska, and above all the 50th State – Hawaii. In Hawaii you will find the famous waves of Waimea, Pipeline or Sunset Beach. In California you surf the waves of Trestles, Rincon, Malibu and Mavericks.

The West Coast

The west coast of the USA has waves all year round. In summer the southerly swells, which can often be inconsistent, reach the coast and in winter the northerly swells produce some of the biggest waves around. The best time for surfing is winter. You will often find kelp floating on the surface smoothing it and leading to glassy conditions all day long. Surf spots are found all along the whole coastline. California has the best-known spots, and is recognised still as the origin of surf culture. Its coast has the greatest surfing population in the world. You will meet surfers here from all walks of life. It is here that you will find tons of surf shops, surfing magazines, surfing videos, surf forecasts and so on and so forth, like nowhere else on the surfing planet. The whole American surfing industry is based in California. A complete industry has been built up around the sport of surfing, and finding a secret spot here is like a miracle happening. Nevertheless there are some great waves and the level of surfing in the water is often exceptional.

The best way to explore the waves of California is to rent a car or buy one, and drive slowly up or down the coastline. You will find value for money motels and fast-food chains on each corner.

California has so many surf spots that to try to describe each one would take up a whole new book. For now we want to name a few highlight spots on the coast. We recommend that once you arrive, you visit the first surf shop and buy yourself a Californian surf guide.

We will begin our journey in San Diego and end up in San Francisco under the Golden Gate Bridge. The first spot worth naming is Windansea in La Jolla, a part of San Diego town. Here you will find a peak breaking on a stony sea bottom with a hollow left and right, and a pretty lively local scene. We go on further in the direction of Blacks. Here, there is a steep, hollow wave that produces nice tubes when the swell is up and the wind is blowing in the right direction. This place lies at the foot of the steep coastline between San Diego and Encinitas, and is not so easy to find.

The next stop is Swami's at the entrance to the town of Encinitas. There is a good peak breaking on a sandy bottom dotted with rocks. By the way, Encinitas is also the home of two good friends, Benno and Jeano. With a great eye for detail, they have brought the legendary, classically styled Beachcruiser surf-bike to life again under the brand name Electra. Check them out in their shop in Leucadia. Of course, both of them know where the best waves are, so a visit can be well worthwhile.

The journey goes on past San Onofre directly to Trestles – one of the most famous spots in California. Just before you drive into San Clemente, you have to park your car and take a long track down to the beach. There are two waves – one in Upper Trestles and the other in Lower Trestles. Both are excellent waves and Trestles is usually packed with people. On towards Los Angeles, you come to Newport with its many stone piers. Newport has some of the best beach breaks that you will find in California.

"Surf City", Huntington Beach, lies next door to Newport. Directly on Huntington Pier is where the best waves are breaking and the famous Op Pro contest is held here annually. In LA itself a surfer shoudn't waste much time. A day is enough to do the short LA-city tour, Sunset Boulevard, Melrose Road, Beverly Hills, Hollywood, Venice Beach and – come on get out of the town! Just behind LA there's Malibu, one of the most historical spots in the world. This is where the surfing culture began in the '60s. Surfers, such as Micky Dora, riding the Malibu waves with their large longboards, became surfing legends here.

Today It is difficult to surf on a wave in Malibu without 10 other surfers already being on it. Onwards, avoiding Oxnard with its stupid localism –

where vandalised boards and car break-ins are quite common – you reach Rincon the most well-known point break in California. Going north from Rincon the water gets colder, the waves larger and the crowd smaller. On the road towards San Francisco, It is worthwhile stopping off for a surf-check in Morro Bay, Monterey and Santa Cruz. Above all you will find the infamous spot Steamer Lane (sharks and locals), which lies directly at the foot of a cliff. Everywhere around here you will find a mixture of point and beach breaks and cold water. Your way leads to Mavericks, one of the better known big-wave spots of the past years. The tragic death of the Hawaiian Mark Foo here in the winter of 94/95 has made this spot additionally legendary. Mark Foo was killed here on a relatively – for Mavericks – "small" day in 18-foot waves. In winter, the best big-wave riders meet here to battle the 20 to 30-foot waves of Mavericks.

Without a doubt, California is one of the best surfing regions in the world, and a surfing trip along its coast is definitely worthwhile.

A lonely break in Northern California (Photo: Roland Hansky)

Hawaii

Hawaii – the mention of the name simply, and justifiably, makes the blood course the blood through the veins of every surfer. Hawaii is the surfing nirvana, it is the crème de la crème, numero uno, No.1. Got it? The surfing season lasts the whole year round. The islands are open to swells from all directions. The State of Hawaii consists of eight island, one of which is called Hawaii. The main surfing islands are Oahu, Maui, Kauai and Hawaii itself. The dream island for surfers, however, is Oahu with its capital Honolulu. The best waves of Hawaii break on Oahu's famous North-Shore. If you go to Hawaii, the North Shore of Oahu is where you want to be. On this short 20 km strip of coast you will find the waves with all the well-known names such as Pipeline, Sunset Beach, Waimea Bay, Haleiwa etc. There is hardly any other place that has so many famous and different waves as this short stretch. You can surf on Oahu in summer as well as winter.

In summer the breaks on the South Shore of the island come alive. The waves are generated by groundswells coming from the southern hemisphere. The surf is good but rather inconsistent. The South Shore, where Honolulu lies, is known by the locals as "Town", while the North Shore is called "Country". A well-known surfing company has adopted this as its trade mark – "Town & Country".

Around Honolulu there are several surf spots. Here you will find the Ala Moana Bowl, a big left-handed tube off Ala Moana Beach Park; other popular spots are Kaisers, Populars, the longboard waves of Waikiki-beach, and last but not least Suicides and Lighthouse off Diamond Head. The real reason why surfers go to Hawaii is the winter wonderland on the North Shore. This is because in winter huge swells come rolling in to the Hawaiian Islands from the north and northwest. Storms in the north Pacific create large swells that sometimes run for thousands of miles until they crash down onto the Hawaiian reefs. These storms bring the famous North Shore of Oahu to life for five months of the year. Particularly in December there is hardly another place on earth where you will find so many surfers in one spot. The season lasts from November to March. It is advisable to avoid the main season in December, unless of course you want to see the Pipeline Masters (one of the most spectacular contests in professional surfing). During this time the waves are gigantic and the water is packed with professional surfers as the pro tour ends and the world champion is crowned. During this time it can be hard to find a bed to sleep in. Apart from that, the waves are usually too large on most days for the average surfer. We recommend that you visit Hawaii from January onwards. The pros have left, and you will be able to find accommodation, and the raging ocean will calm down at least a little. You do not need to be afraid that there will not be any waves left for you. At the end you will go home knowing that you will have ridden some of the biggest waves in your surfing life. The waves rarely drop below 6 feet at this time of year. You can easily leave your shortboard at home. The waves in Hawaii are very powerful, and you will certainly need at least a seven-foot board or even a few inches longer.

International flights all land in Honolulu. You can already get ready to be shocked when you see the famous Waikiki Beach – thousands of tourists on a small stretch of sand with a concrete jungle as a backdrop. Did someone speak of paradise? It is an American big city, just like any other. The best thing to do is to hire a car straight away and drive out to the North Shore. The journey will take you about 45 minutes, and you can find good accommodation there. A good tip is to go to Foodland Store – a supermarket, which lies just behind Waimea Bay. Here you will find a notice board with offers of private lodgings on it. When we were there we found a cheap apartment costing US $10 a day per person this way. An alternative is the Backpackers, which belonged to Mark Foo. You will find this directly behind Waimea Bay as you come from the direction of Haleiwa. A dormitory bed space here will cost you around US $15.

There are a lot of great waves on the North Shore. Right from the beginning you should buy yourself a surf guide from one of the surf shops.

We recommend the "Surfer's Guide to Hawaii" by Greg Ambrose. In this you will find all the details about currents, sea bottoms, wind directions etc. It also covers the islands of Maui, Kauai and Hawaii. For now we just want to cover a few of the more interesting spots on the North Shore. The surfing wonderland starts directly on Haleiwa Alií Beach Park. The waves break on a stony bottom and give you a quick, sometimes hollow, right-hander and a short left-hander. When the swell is big, the current is very strong and will pull you away from the shoulder right onto the peak. Take a comfortable little drive down the North Shore and stop next at Laniakea. This is a fantastic right reefbreak with many hollow sections allowing rides of up to 400 metres. Now you arrive at the next spots: Jocko's and Chun's, which are right next to each other. Jocko's is a quick hollow left-hander, which has everything in it from 4-foot fun waves to pitching 10-footers. Chun's has one of the easiest waves on the North Shore. It is mainly a right but there is also

High season on the North Shore (Photo: Joli)

a short left. Chun's can handle waves from 2 to 8 feet and is the perfect place to get to know the North Shore. Two days here and you are ready to move on. The next stop brings you to the No. 1 big-wave spot – Waimea Bay. The waves here are really only for the experts. Just stand on the cliff and watch the spectacle. With ten surfers on one 30-foot wave, this is no place for you. It is really serious stuff here, and not even all the professionals surf here when it is big. So keep your fingers off and just watch! Passing by spots like Rockpile and Log Cabins, the road leads in the direction of the best known 300 metres of beach in the surfing world. Directly opposite the Sunset Beach Elementary School is where you find it – the "Banzai Pipeline". This is the ultimate left-hand tube of this world. The right-hander on the same wave called "Backdoor" and is by no means any less awesome. Pipeline is the benchmark for all other tubes. It breaks onto a reef in extremely shallow water close to the beach. It is the most dangerous wave in the world, and here you cannot afford to make any mistakes. A wipe-out in big waves can end with a serious injury. You should never hang around in the impact zone – duck-diving is virtually impossible. Pipeline breaks from between 4 to 20 feet. At 15 feet plus it starts breaking further out on the so-called second reef. No matter how often you have seen the wave in pictures or on video, nothing can prepare you for the real thing. Even the Hawaiians do not play this wave down. At the end of December the "Pipemasters" takes place here – the last competition in the year. Moving on past Rocky Point, a peak with a left and a right-hander, you come to the third jewel of the North Shore – Sunset Beach with its sensational right-hander. After a steep drop and a flatter middle section there is a thick tube on the inside. Sunset breaks some 800 metres out to sea from between 4 to 20 feet. You can easily paddle out through a channel. But watch out for the notorious west peaks. They often break right across the channel. Everyone will get caught inside at Sunset one day or the other. Just on from Sunset you reach the spot with the name of Velzeyland, a peak for locals-only that breaks from between 3 to 7 feet. And, you have now reached the end of the North Shore. How long did that take? 25 minutes? It is unbelievable how many spots lie along this short stretch. So let's turn around and start all over again. If you stop anywhere along the North Shore to go surfing, do not leave any valuables in the car. Unfortunately we had to learn this lesson ourselves by having a video camera stolen once.

The surf-check in Hawaii is very important. Take a good look at where you enter the water, and do not underestimate the size and power of the waves. Always remember that conditions in Hawaii can change very rapidly. You paddle out to some 6-foot waves, and three sets later they are already coming in at 8-foot. Sometimes the swell can double itself within an hour. If you are in Hawaii during the main season, there will often be days when the waves are too big for the average surfer. But be patient, there will also be days when the waves are around 4 to 8 feet , and you will have some unbelievable rides.

In Hawaii, the local scene is very, very lively, and, as a non-Hawaiian, you should steer clear of some spots e.g., Makaha on the Westside or Velzeyland on the North Shore. So, remember, behave when you are in the water and treat the locals with the respect they deserve.

The other islands also offer some great surfing, particularly Maui. This is actually more well-known for its windsurfing, particularly at Hookipa Beach. The best waves in Maui are at Honolua Bay in the north of the island, where there is a long peeling, right-hand point break which works from 3 to 20-foot. Another wave, called Peahi, better known as Jaws, has become well-known for tow-in surfing in mega waves. The surfer is dragged behind a jetski like water skier and pulled into waves that he would otherwise not be able to paddle into. They use specially designed boards with foot straps to avoid being bounced off at high speed. Surfers such as Laird Hamilton, Pete Carbrinha, Darrick Doerner and Dave Kalama with their combination of surfing and windsurfing skills, have entered a new dimension of big wave surfing. At Jaws, waves in the 30 to 40 foot range have successfully been ridden.

Hawaii is a real surfing paradise, and It is definitely well worth a trip to go surfing here. So you should better start practising holding your breath in the bath. Aloha!

"Mister Pipeline" himself – Gerry Lopez (Photo: Kuta Lines Australia)

4   Australia

Australia, Down-under, Oz, or however you call it, is the dreamland of every surfer. The whole of the east coast with its spots such as Kirra and Bells, the south coast with Cactus, and the west coast with Margret River and the Box make this place, kilometre after kilometre, and spot after spot, an absolute surfers' paradise. The focus however, is on the east coast with its centres of population in Melbourne, Sydney and Brisbane. It is highly likely that you will make your first contact with Australian waves along here because this is where the best-known spots are. The fantastic thing about Australia is the great variety of waves that you find there.

In Australia you will always find a protected bay or peninsula where there are clean waves breaking in a sheltered area. Although you can find some real monster waves as well, it rarely gets over 8 to 10 feet.

Nevertheless there are some waves that can be really gnarly, particularly on reefs. You will have to get used to having to enter and exit the water over rocks and the like. Many waves break next to cliffs or rocks. Therefore a thorough surf check is always a must.

The planning for your journey will naturally be dependent on the season of the year. In the Australian winter (June to October) the waves come in from the south and from the west. Southern Australia, Western Australia as well as the east coast have cold but powerful waves during this time. Although the climate cannot exactly be called a real winter, a full suit will be necessary.

In summer (November to February), the Australians have to struggle along with often smaller waves and onshore winds. However, there are often one or two summer swells. In the period between February to April, just off the far northeast coast, areas of low-pressure build up and create so-called cyclones. If you ever catch a cyclone swell, you will never forget it.

From about Sydney upwards to a bit above Brisbane, the whole east coast becomes one large surf spot. While you will find the best waves at the famous spots such as Kirra or Burleigh Heads, you just would not believe how many good waves there are along the coast during a cyclone swell. And because at this time the height of summer has just past, you will not need a wetsuit because the water is still at a comfortable temperature. At all costs, you need a surf guidebook that will tell you when which spots are working and where to find them. In our opinion, the best book in this respect is the "Surfing and Sailboarding Guide to Australia" by Nat Young. The edition we have is rather old, and we do not know whether it is still in print. Another surf guidebook, with lots of great photos in it, is the one by Mark Warren and is simply called "Mark Warren's Surf Guide to Australia".

For your first surfing trip we can recommend the following itinerary: take a flight after the end of January to Sydney, buy or hire a car, rattle around the area of Sydney for a few days, and then drive up the coast northwards. On the way you will pass by some wonderful beaches and picturesque surf spots. We recommend this programme because we think that for the newcomer to Australia it offers all that he could ever dream of: sun, warm water and good waves.

On the second trip to Australia, you can easily give the power waves of the Australian winter or autumn in Victoria or Southern Australia a try, or go on a surfari in the lonely region of Western Australia. There are numerous possibilities. Just like Arnold Schwarzenegger says in Terminator I, "I'll be back".

There is a sense of localism or even local patriotism here, despite, of course the generally friendly and open attitude you meet in Australia. Just a word about the notorious sharks. In Australia there are many sharks, but they only present a danger in rare cases. Above all it is the loners – the white shark and the tiger shark – that are a threat to humans in the colder waters of Southern and Western Australia. Here, any intruder in their stamping ground is considered to be potential food. The smaller types of shark live mostly in swarms and have generally something better to do than attack such a large animal as the human being. If you want to play safe, do not go surfing at dawn or dusk. At these times of day Mr and Mrs Shark are dining. If you spot a shark in the water, take the next wave lying on your belly back to the beach (this way you will not fall off). Counting all of our trips together, we have spent probably more than three years in Australia, sometimes in some out-of-the-way places, but we have only seen sharks in the water twice, and they were somehow much more interested in the ten million other fish in the water. On closer examination most of the sharks turned out to be non other than our friend 'Flipper', who is quite common in Australia, and who loves to join the surfers in the water.

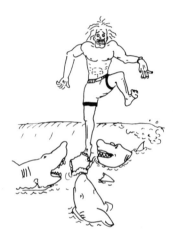

"Bon appetit!"
(Drawing: Stefan „Muli" Müller)

Victoria (March–October)

In Australian, Victoria means "big, powerful waves" (just kidding). You should look for these in winter and autumn around the town of Torquay. Torquay is a real surfing Mecca and the base for firms such as Rip Curl and Quiksilver. Next to it is the famous spot Bells Beach with its long big waves and the legendary surfing championships at Easter. But it is not only Bells that gets the adrenaline flowing. Just next door you have Winkipop, and in any case the whole area around Torquay is full of unbelievable waves. Seek and ye shall find!

Aussie Barrel
(Photo: Joli)

New South Wales (All Year round)

The centre of NSW is Sydney. Although It is a big city with millions of inhabitants, there are some beautiful beaches and quality surf spots. The well-known spots are Manly, Bondi and in particular North Narabeen. Narabeen is north of Sydney and has produced several world famous surfers. The main surf spot is at the northern end of the beach – hence the name. Although It is only a beach break, the quality of the waves can be fantastic. But since it is still a city beach, it is usually very crowded, and there is a firm, laid-down pecking order: the locals on top and the tourists underneath. Further to the north of the town are Freshwater and Avalon (reefbreaks). You can simply drive along the shoreline and check all the spots, one after the other. However, before your journey takes you further up north, you should spend a few days on the south coast of NSW. Start from the industrial town of Wollongong in the south just below Sydney. A stop-off here is well worth it, not only because of the waves around Wollongong (Woonona and Sandon Point are a couple of names as an idea for you to start with). If you need a new board or some other equipment, you should check out the surf shop run by the Byrne brothers. Two of the brothers are ex-pro surfers, the third, Phil Byrne, is the well-known shaper who made Tom Caroll's boards.

The brothers not only sell top-class boards, they are also happy to give you tips about where the best surfing conditions are at the time. As soon as you drive southwards out of Wollongong you begin to meet the breathtaking nature of the south coast with kangaroos and everything that goes with it: one spot after the other.

The Australian Pipeline is worth a special mention. The spot lies in an aborigine reservation, and they have the absolute last word here in the water. If you do not show respect, you will soon be sent back to the beach with the words "I think you better go in" – in other words – get out. Leave the waves to the aborigines where they want them and you will have a great session. This left-hander breaks perfectly, and the tube is almost always open. About 15 km south of the town Nowra is the turn off to Jervis Bay. Follow this road to Wreck Bay. Somewhere along the route you will come across the signpost "Summercloud Bay", which you must follow. Park the car and then walk for about 20 minutes through the bush until you reach the Pipeline. Take a good look at the entry and exit points as this will save a few cuts and bruises getting in and out of the water.

Back up in Sydney just drive on the Pacific Highway northwards. The water and the weather get warmer the farther you go north. All along the route you will find top-class surf spots.

You should really make a stop in Crescent Head (long right-hand point break and a local pub with good food) as well as further north in Yamba. Just outside Yamba is Angourie Point called "Anga".

This is a very beautiful stretch of land in a national park with superb waves. Oh yes, by the way, the entry point into the water at the tip of the peninsula can be pretty hairy in big surf. Good timing and avoiding slipping or stumbling on the slippery ground when you race into the water is important.

The next world-class wave on your way northwards is the right-hander at Lennox Head. This is one of the many point breaks in Australia where a good wave here is worth twenty elsewhere. But take care the waves break on an unforgiving rocky bottom.

From here it is only a few kilometres to Byron Bay – the pilgrimage destination of all backpacker tourists in Australia. There is a lot going on here, not only in the bars but also out in the surf. During the 70s Byron Bay was the favourite spot for many surfers, who sought the alternative

A high standard of surfing on the beaches around Sydney (Photo: Joli)

lifestyle. The best known wave in the area is the long right-hand point break called the "Pass", directly on the south side of the large bay.

From here you go in the direction of Queensland, the next state full of waves.

Queensland (October to April)

Queensland begins north of the Tweed River, and the action starts just across the border. The southern part of Queensland is also called the Gold Coast, and this really tells the story. If you ever experience a cyclone swell here, you will wake up at night stammering the words "Kirra, Burleigh, Snapper ... cyclone" for the rest of your life.

Duranbah is one of the best beach breaks in Australia and lies directly on the border with NSW. The standard of surfing in the water is extremely high. It is so high that even some of the surf pros do not stand out particularly. This beach break has fire.

Just over the hill are the famous Queensland point breaks around the town of Coolangatta. Starting with Snapper Rocks it connects directly into Rainbow Bay and Greenmount. They are actually three separate spots, but if the swell is large enough, they combine into one single dream ride. However, each of the spots is a fantastic wave on Its own. The strong currents are a typical characteristic of these points. The current is often so strong that you have trouble staying in one spot.

From Greenmount its only one hundred metres north to the legendary Kirra Point – probably the best and longest right-hand tube, and it breaks on sand. The wave starts to break on an artificially built stone pier and continues down the point. The current here is at least as strong as in Greenmount, and the principle is easy: into the water, paddle, surf and then on land, run back up to the point again. When Kirra is pumping there are rarely less than 50 people in the water. Once, we counted as many as 100 surfers in the water even at 5 o'clock in the morning. But because of the strong current and the length of the wave, sometime or the other you will catch a wave yourself. Since the wave is seemingly endless, you can wait further down the line for the opportunity that a surfer will not make the tube or will fall off during a manoeuvre. This strategy is not so bad because the outside, where the wave begins to break, is usually filled up by locals who know the wave inside out. But take care when you paddle into a wave. The locals are real masters of the tube and often, just when it seems that the surfer will never make it out of the tube, they prove you wrong and come flying out of the barrel. So, do not take-off unless you are 200% sure that the surfer has wiped-out. Do not drop in!

Further along the coast you come to Burleigh Heads which is another right-hand point break, which offers long clean tubes on a sandy bottom. When the swell is big, Burleigh is generally better than Kirra, but despite its sandy bottom you should not underestimate this wave.

Past the casino and party-town "Surfer's Paradise" (seriously this is really the name of this town, and there actually are some good beach breaks), you go in the direction of Noosa Heads – a further highlight in Australia. The countryside is already very tropical, and in the Noosa Heads National Park you find once again bay after bay with long, clean point break waves. Under the right conditions Noosa is one of the best waves in Australia.

If you travel up and down the east coast, the west coast and the south coast of Australia you are likely to find a new spot which only works under particular conditions every time you go. If you have experienced some of the waves we described above, you too will surely become a human boomerang that keeps coming back. See you later mate!

Two sensational waves – Greenmount (in the foreground) and Kirra Point (in the background by the stone pier) (Photo: Joli)

5   South Pacific

T he islands of the South Pacific belong to the most beautiful spots in the world. After our trip through this region, we can understand why there was a Mutiny on the Bounty. Our tour took us through Fiji, The Cook Islands and Tahiti. However, the other island groups such as Tonga or Samoa also have fantastic waves. If you do not want to discover the islands on your own, you can book a yacht tour. The experienced provider of these yacht tours is the Australian Surf Travel Company (STC). The best time for a trip to the South Pacific is between April and October. The swells are created by storms in the Tasmanian Sea, The Coral Sea and Antarctica.

Fiji

If you go to Fiji to surf, you will only have one wave in mind – "Cloudbreak". It is one of the best lefts in the world. Every year, hundreds of surfers from all over the world come to Fiji just to ride this wave. Like the "Pipeline" in Hawaii, surfers always speak in awe of this wave. We were able to confirm this: after two weeks – with a group of just ten surfers, we had ten broken boards, a broken arm, ripped leashes, reef dings in the boards and several more or less serious reef cuts. "Cloudbreak" is a fast hollow left reef break. The wave lies in the middle of the ocean, on a coral reef, and can only be reached by boat. Dependent on where you are staying you need between 15-30 minutes by boat to get there.

It is important to book accommodation in advance on Fiji. You can choose between two alternatives, whereby with one of these alternatives, while you can still surf on good waves, you are not allowed to surf "Cloudbreak". Sounds crazy but It is true. In Fiji the fishing and surfing rights of a reef belong to a particular family. In the case of "Cloudbreak", there is an argument between one of the villages and the American owners of a surf camp that has acquired the rights. Quarrels and armed clashes have increased in the last few years. The courts are currently handling the case. The situation changes constantly, and you should enquire in advance where you can get a boat, which is at all allowed to take you out.

International flights all land in Nadi. If you have already booked accommodation in advance, arrange to be picked up from the airport. You do not need a car on Fiji. If you have not booked in advance, ask about one of the possibilities listed below in a travel office at the airport. Your choice is limited to one of the two surfing camps: Tavarua or Namotu. Both of these lie on small private islands, which only have these camps. Tavarua is probably the best known surf camp on Fiji. For about US $ 150 per day, you live full-board with all meals and boat rides included.

The boat takes you out to the break and anchors in the channel while you surf for 3-4 hours. It is a good idea to bring something to eat and drink with you on the boat. "Cloudbreak" is a radical wave. It breaks onto a flat reef shelf and can provide rides up to 100 metres. When the wave hits the reef, the lip pitches forward at least as far as the wave is high.

The feeling when you make the drop and the lip pounds down on the reef by the side of you or when you stand in the barrel is hard to describe in words. Pure adrenaline! If you wipe-out, however, you are likely to hit the sharp reef and you may suddenly find yourself standing in knee-deep water.

There is no duck-diving any more as the water is far to shallow. At this point you are at the mercy of the waves. Just do the starfish and let

Cloudbreak (Photo: Jeff Hornbaker, Quiksilver)

yourself be washed to the side and into the channel, and be thankful when you escape with only a few scratches. It is better not to take the first wave of a set, because if you do not make it, or if it closes down further down the line (this hardly ever happens though), the next wave in the set will mercilessly eat you alive.

The shoulder is relatively safe, and even if the waves are too big for you to surf, you should paddle out onto the shoulder. You will surely receive the biggest adrenaline rush of your life when you feel and see the power and size of these waves. Besides that you will never forget the picture of a surfer with outstretched arms in the biggest tube you have ever seen. Watch out, however, for boomer-sets that swing wide and will knock you off the shoulder. Even on smaller days "Cloudbreak" is a breathtaking wave. It breaks with unbelievable perfection.

If possible at all do go to Fiji. Besides the fantastic waves you will meet some of the friendliest people on this planet. The Fijians take things pretty easy. They have their own time – Fiji time. Never be in a hurry as everything goes a little slowly here. The most important word on Fiji is "Bula". It means simply "Hello". Everyone you meet greets you with a friendly Bula. So, on that note "Bula, Bula!"

Tahiti

*T*his is the absolute South Sea paradise. These French-Polynesian islands are everything you would imagine about a South Sea paradise: white sand, blue lagoons, dolphins and perfect waves. The well-known islands for surfing are Tahiti itself, Moorea and Huahine. Huahine has one of the very few right-handers in the French-Polynesian island group. However the local scene is rumoured to be a bit of a worry and does not particularly welcome the surfing tourists. So, you should focus on the other two islands. The most famous spot on the main island is Teahupoo which made it into the surf magazines with its gnarly grinding tubes. If "Pipeline" in Hawaii is starting to feel a bit boring, try Teahupoo to get the blood pressure up again. Moorea has some slightly less radical, but equally perfect waves. The islands get their swells from the Antarctic storms which come up from the southwest.

Prices on Tahiti are, however, anything but cheap. For a simple night's stay you will easily have to pay US $ 50. A car hire will cost you a quick US $ 80 a day. You cannot even get a pizza for less than US $ 15. The main town of Papeete is particularly dear. It is enough if you spend the first and last night there. Our tip is to hop on the ferry to Moorea straight away, which goes several times a day. In any case one of the best waves in the region – the left-hand reef break at Haapiti – breaks on Moorea. Apart from the many luxury resorts, a few hundred metres past the Club Med, there is also a backpackers hostel and a camping ground, still not exactly cheap, but there is not much else to choose from.

Moorea has about six spots, of which Haapiti is the Number 1. Haapiti is roughly in the middle on the west side of the island. It is not easy to find though.

Look out for a small concrete landing pier built out into the water. From there It is about a half-an-hour's paddle over the lagoon to the reef passage that the wave breaks into. It is not unusual to have dolphins accompany you across the lagoon. If you are really lucky a local may even give you a lift in his boat which saves a lot of paddling. Just before you reach the reef passage a current will pull you out to sea. On your trip to the South Pacific, in general it is a good idea to bring a pair of binoculars with you so that you can estimate from the shore how high the waves are. At Haapiti, you will be surprised how high the waves actually are when you are across the lagoon and are paddling close up to the reef. Haapiti works in a southwest swell and from 4 to 12 feet. French-Polynesia is an amazing but expensive paradise. If you accept this fact and budget for it, you will have a great time surfing some of the bluest and cleanest barrels in the world.

6 Indonesia, Mexico and the Rest of the World

Indonesia

Indonesia consists of about 12,000 islands with countless numbers of waves. Most of the surfers who come to Indonesia, however, go to Bali. Since the 70s, Bali attracts surfing (and other) tourists from all over the world, above all the Australians, as it is really just around the corner for them. Over the last years, the more adventurous have begun to explore the other islands to get away from the crowds in Bali. Numerous new spots have been discovered, and several surf camps have sprung up. For information over the whole region, including Bali, we recommend the surfing guide "Indo Surf & Lingo". It contains all that is worth knowing about the Indonesian surf spots, some information about the culture and the most useful Indonesian words. English, by the way, does not get you very far outside of Bali.

In Indonesia the dry season begins in May and ends in August. During this time the action is at the spots on the west side of Bali, particularly the famous waves of Uluwatu and Padang Padang. They come from the big low pressure systems far off in the Indian Ocean. On top of that, during this time, the prevailing winds are from the southeast which create offshore conditions that often last the whole day. On a good day you will find 50-100 surfers in the water at Uluwatu. To get away from these crowds you will have to flee to another Indonesian Island like for example the islands of Java and Sumatra in the west, or the easterly islands such as Lombok, Sumbawa or West Timor, or book a yacht trip with STC through the Mentawai islands off Sumatra.

The rainy season, on the other hand, often brings big waves and offshore conditions from west winds on the east side of Bali. During this time the waves break in Sanur and Nusa Dua. The season begins in December and ends at the beginning of March. On Bali you have all sorts of waves to choose from. For example you can surf beach breaks, only a few though, at Kuta and Legian. If you are looking for reef breaks, you can have razor-sharp ones, extremely shallow ones and deeper, not so dangerous ones. This of course depends largely on the size of the waves.

In Bali, you can surf waves from 2 to around 12 feet. But you do not have to necessarily stick to the main seasons mentioned above to find good conditions. The transition periods between the dry and rainy seasons also produce good waves, but the weather is somewhat inconsistent. People say that you can surf everyday on Bali somewhere on at least a 2 feet wave all year round.

In the dry season, Kuta is the place to stay. Here you can always find a reasonably priced hotel, and buy a meal like grilled fish with lots of garlic for around US $ 5. There are all sorts of things to do in the evening; play pool, watch surfing videos in one of the many bars or party through the night in a club. A cool bar is the "Tubes Surfer's Bar" where there is a tide chart on the wall which will tell at what time you have to get up in the morning to catch the first barrel. In the "Tubes Bar" you can also book into the Garajigang (G-Land) Surf Camp. The airport where the international flights land is called Denpassar (the capital of Bali) but actually is in Kuta. The best thing is to get a taxi and let it take you directly into town and look for a hotel near the beach and the airport. Here you will have several Surf spots directly on your doorstep. Apart from these few breaks in Kuta, the best waves are in the south of Bali, about an hour from Kuta. It is therefore necessary to hire a car or a motorcycle in Kuta.

Directly in Kuta and Legian there are some good surf spots. On the side of the runway built out into the water there are the two spots Airport Rights and Lefts. You can get tubed while the jumbos thunder through the sky above you. If you prefer a beach break to adjust to the conditions, you can try the waves on Kuta Beach and Legian Beach. They are both good beach breaks with steep, hollow waves. The best-known wave on Bali, Uluwatu, is in the south near the temple with the same name. Next to this are two spots Padang Padang (double because its twice as good) and Bingin. All three waves are extremely fast, hollow and break in shallow water over coral reefs. To get to Uluwatu it takes you an hour on a bumpy, muddy and stony track, of which brings you out on to the point of a cliff (by the time you read this there will probably be a new road, just see for yourself). From here you walk down a narrow path past several 'warungs' built into the rocks. In those little huts you can get tasty food – recommended are Nasi Goreng and fruit salad. After your surf session you can simply lie down and relax, or get a massage as you watch the other surfers pull into tube after tube. To get into the water you have to climb down a ladder into a cave. At low tide you can walk out of the cave, but at high tide you will have to paddle out. Surf boots are absolutely essential. Uluwatu may not be an easy wave, but if you make the drop and race along the wall as the lip is flying over your head, and you manage to find

How much is a week in G-land worth? (Photo: Tony King, Surf Travel Co.)

the light at the end of the tunnel, then everything else, the bumpy road, the crowds and the runs are forgotten. You will find the same kind of conditions in Padang Padang and Bingin. Padang is somewhat gnarlier and only breaks when the swell is around 6 foot plus i.e., when Uluwatu is out of control. On Bali, however, the surf is not only dependent on the swell or the wind. It is essential to know when high and low tide is. Some spots are simply unsurfable when the tide is out.

Finally, a few words about the other Indonesian islands. In the last few years, above all, two waves have become popular. One is the right-hander in Lagundri Bay on Nias Island, which lies just off the coast of Sumatra. Accommodation and food is cheap and the waves are cooking, literally. The water and air temperature is very warm. Malaria can be a problem, so go prepared. The other wave is on the south-east tip of Java at a place called Garajigang, also known as G-Land. For several years now there is a surf camp in G-Land, and for a few years now, one of the competitions of the Professional World Tour takes place there. G-Land breaks best during the dry season and works between 4 to 12 feet. It is a kind of left-hand point break/reef break, which runs through four main sections, some of them really dish out some grinding barrels. G- Land is a perfect but intimidating wave when it is big. To get there you have to fly to Denpassar on Bali and take a boat from Jimbaran Bay to Plengkung. The only place to stay is in a surf camp for about US $ 75 per night all inclusive. Both G-Land and Nias are not easy to reach, and in particular the road to Nias is a real adventure by itself. These days this unfortunately does not guarantee that the waves will not be crowded.

The water in Indonesia is warm so you will not need a wetsuit. Nevertheless, you should pack a wetshirt to protect yourself from the strong sun. To make yourself understood you should remember the following two sentences: "Terima kasih" – 'Thank you' or 'No, thank you', and, "Saya cari ombak-ombak besar" - 'I'm looking for big waves'.

The right at Nias: sticky hot, malaria etc., but worth it (Photo: Joli)

Mexico

Mexico offers two alternatives for the surf hungry traveller. There is the Baja California and the mainland of Mexico. All spots are on the Pacific Coast, with the exception of Veracruz in the Gulf of Mexico. In the summer months the spots receive swell from the tropical cyclones which come up from the south. In winter the swell is generated by storms in the North Pacific off the coast of Mexico. By the way these are the same storms which pound the north shore of Hawaii in winter. There are surfers, who surf the swell in Hawaii, and then fly off to Mexico to ride on practically the same swell further south. In summer you should choose the southern tip of the Baja or the mainland of Mexico. In winter you surf the northern part of the Baja. The spots directly on the US American-Mexican border are packed full at the weekends. Mexico has every type of wave: from the absolute mind-blowing big wave spot on Todos Santos Island to the sand dredging tubes of Puerto Escondido, and the point breaks such as "Shipwrecks" near Cabo San Lucas. Cabo San Lucas is a popular party town with American surfers and marlin fishers. It lies on the southern tip of the Baja. Finding somewhere to stay overnight is not difficult. There is also no lack of surf spots and night clubs around the neighbourhood of Cabo. Do not miss the "Cabo Wabo" and the "Squid Roe". There is an absolutely awesome wave breaking in the north of the Baja on the island of Todos Santos, which lies just off Ensenada. With its name "Killers", it hits the nail right on the head. You can only reach this by boat. Here is where the big wave riders meet annually to charge at the 20-foot plus monster waves. Last but not least there is the most famous wave on mainland Mexico at Puerto Escondido – the Mexican pipeline. This little fishing village is about 50 minutes by plane or ten hours by bus from Mexico City. The waves break on a sandy bottom at Playa Zicatela. You will think, "Only a beach break!". You could not be more wrong, because the sand is so hard that the waves break like they do on a reef. This is one of the few beach breaks that holds waves up to 12 feet without things getting out of control. In a big swell and with your belly churning you can surf further inside the bay. This means that the closer you get to the harbour, the better your belly will feel. So, "Olas grande!"

The Rest of the World

The "rest of the world" is of course quite an area to cover, and you would not believe where some of the waves are hiding. Just about everyone knows Hawaii, Australia and California. But, who would know that you can surf on the Easter Islands, Lake Michigan, on a river in Munich, on the Typhoon Lagoon in Disneyworld, in the Flowrider Surfpool in Norway, and so on and so forth. Here we have picked but three cherries from the surfing 'cake' which we had the chance to taste. The rest is out there for you to explore.

Costa Rica

osta Rica has good waves all year round. The tropical climate and the warm water make the country a dream destination for surfers. The friendly Ticos (the nickname for Costa Ricans), cheap food and good accommodation all add to this. International flights land at San José. The best thing to do is to hire a car and drive off in the direction of the Pacific. Here you are left with the choice between the two larger places Jaco on the central Pacific coast (about two hours from San José), or Tamarindo in the north (about five hours from San José).

In Costa Rica you have only two seasons in the year, the dry season (December to April) and the rainy season (May to November). Both periods have their advantages and disadvantages. During the rainy season the waves are generally more consistent, the accommodation is cheaper and the spots are less crowded. On the other hand a 4-wheel drive car (not quite cheap to hire) is absolutely essential to negotiate the muddy jungle tracks to the next surf spot. Also some waves are only reachable by boat (e.g., Witches Rock at a price of about US $ 150 per boat). The dry season, on the other hand, has perfect off-shore conditions, better road conditions, and the waves also break on the Caribbean shore. The disadvantages however are overcrowded spots and expensive, often fully booked accommodation. No matter when you are going to Costa Rica, it has got everything you need to put a huge smile on your face.

The Pacific coast is characterised by point breaks and long sandy beaches with sometimes perfect tubes. Similar to Mexico, on this side of Costa Rica, the swell comes up from the south during the dry season, and down from the north during the rainy season. The well-known spots on the Peninsula de Nicoya in the north are Witches Rock (famous through "Endless Summer 2"), the beaches of Tamarindo, Playa Negra and Mal Pais. On the central Pacific coast, Jaco, Playa Hermosa and Quepos offer the best conditions. Further to the south, in the direction of Panama, Dominical and Pavones (one of the longest waves in the Pacific) are worth a mention.

The more protected coastline on the Caribbean side gives you, apart from good beach breaks, also razor-sharp coral reefs, and during the dry season, the biggest waves in town. These are produced by the strong winter storms that travel from the USA through the Gulf of Mexico. During the rainy season, the waves on the Caribbean side are generally smaller, if there is not a hurricane passing through. The best spot in this area is Puerto Viejo (Salsa Brava).

Getting up for the dawn patrol should not be much of a problem, as the good old Costa Rican coffee would wake even the dead.

South Africa

*T*he time to go surfing in South Africa is in spring and summer. The Number One wave spot in South Africa has to be Jeffreys Bay (J-Bay). It is about 100 kilometres south of Port Elizabeth on the east side of South Africa, and is one of the longest and most perfect waves in the world. It breaks onto a sandy covered rock shelf. J-Bay is just like a machine, and produces one perfect wave after the other. Two to three tubes on one wave are possible. J-Bay has two separate waves which sometimes connect with a flatter section in between. When the swell is pumping It is difficult to get out. Getting back in over the rocks is equally as difficult. The water in J-Bay is rather chilly and the strong wind often adds to this. Therefore you should bring a fullsuit and booties. Besides the world-class wave in Jeffreys Bay, the beaches around Durban also have quality waves.

Réunion

*T*he surf spots on Réunion are all concentrated on the west side of the island. There are about 10-12 spots, of which the majority are reef breaks. The swells come in from the south to southwest from the Antarctica and its violent storms. The best time to visit is between June and September. The best wave is St. Leu. This breaks along a shallow reef directly into a bay. Booties are an absolute necessity because the reef is covered with sea urchins. Value for money accommodation is a bit of a problem on Réunion. The beach resorts are extremely expensive and really do not fit into the surfer's budget. Acceptable accommodation can be found in the hills with some of the local families, but then you have the disadvantage of living away from the beach. In St. Leu itself, you either have to camp out under the trees on the beach (sounds better than it really is), or rent an apartment.

The world is covered with surf spots, and actually any land with a coast has waves, whether it be in the Pacific, the Atlantic, the Indian Ocean or in the Mediterranean. Day in, day out, somewhere in the world, a countless number of undiscovered and yet unsurfed waves are breaking. The surfer's eternal dream is to find the secret spot – a perfect wave with no other surfers in sight. Somewhere out there the perfect wave is breaking. You just have to get off your couch, pack your bags and go looking. But wherever you go do not forget to

Surf hard and respect the ocean!

What are you waiting for? (Photo: Tony King, Surf Travel Co.)

The key to success – radical but controlled (Photo: Joli)

V. COMPETITIVE SURFING, SURF LINGO AND INFORMATION

Competitive Surfing

T he professionals surfers are the measure of all things in this sport. They travel around the world and compete at the most famous surf spots in the world (unfortunately not always in the best conditions though). The top 44 pros compete in a series of roughly 14 competitions (the number changes each year) on the ASP World Championship Tour (WCT). The up-and-coming surfers have to collect enough points in the World Qualifying Series (WQS) in order to qualify for the following year's WCT.

In a competition it is all about the most radical manoeuvres on the best waves. "The surfer doing the most radical manoeuvres in the most critical parts of the biggest or best waves over the longest functional distance shall be deemed the winner." Quite simple, eh? On the WCT two pros surf against each other in exactly timed heats. An independent group of judges gives a points score for each ride. Each surfer is only allowed to surf a limited number of waves. Usually the three best rides are taken into account.

There are a number of surfers who can match it with the best in the world, but who are, however, not very successful in competitions. On one hand this is often because they find it hard to surf under competition pressure, and on the other, to fulfil the criteria the judges are looking for. If the surfer falls off during a manoeuvre, irrespective of how radical it was, he does not receive any points for it. A tube ride only counts when the surfer emerges from the tube irrespective of how long he had been in the tube before. This means that professional surfers have to develop a radical, but nevertheless controlled surfing style for competitions. Being able to find the right balance is the stumbling block for many a young hot rookie.

However, pro-surfing has produced a number of great surfers over the years. Here are a few that we think you should know:

Kelly Slater (USA)

The six-times World Champion – who can only be beaten by Flipper. Had a role in Baywatch and is the pop star of the surfing tour. He can do everything – big waves, tubes, small wave tricks etc.

Tom Curren (USA)

In the 1980's he was three-times World Champion. Is a master of the smooth style and competition strategy. He has the ultimate touch. Once, someone described him by saying "Tom Curren is the ocean".

Tom Carroll (Aus)

Twice World Champion. No one surfs powerful waves like he does. He matches power with power. His surfing at "Pipeline" belongs to the best ever.

Mark Occilupo (Aus)

The freak. He always had the misfortune in the 1980's to have to compete against Tom Curren, and therefore missed out on the World Championship. Curren has now retired, but 'Occy' came back and battled it out with the new schoolers to become the 1999 world champion. Well done mate!

Lisa Andersen (USA)

One of the most radical female surfers ever. Surfs hard, wins the Championship and is at the same time a mother. Cool.

Surf Lingo

360: A 360 (three-sixty) degree turn on the wave

Aerial: A manoeuvre where the surfer launches off the lip of the wave, is airborne for a short moment, and lands back on the wave

Backside: (to surf on the backhand) Surfing with one's back to the wave face

Barrel: See Tube

Beach break: Waves breaking on sand

Big waves: Large waves over 10 feet

Board bag: A protective travel bag for the surfboard

Bodyboarder: Also called a Boogie boarder. A surfer who rides a short soft foam board lying down or kneeling

Boomer: A wave larger than the average size on a particular day in a group of waves (also boomer-set)

Bottom-turn: A turn at the bottom of the wave face

Break: Area in the water where a wave breaks. Also a general expression for surfing beach (surf spot)

Carving: Surfing through a turn on the rails of the surfboard, (also as a compliment; this guy is carving).

Catch a rail: To lose balance during a manoeuvre caused by incidentally digging the rail into the wave

Caught inside: An incoming set breaks in front of the surfer who has to dive or duck-dive through it

Channel: Area where no waves are breaking due to deep water or a current. Also grooves on the underside of the board designed to increase speed.

Chops: Uneven, whipped up surface on the water

Close-out: A wave that breaks along its whole length simultaneously – not ideal for surfing

Crowd: Large number of surfers in the water

Custom-made: A surfboard designed and shaped particularly for the individual

Cutback: A turn that takes the surfer back from the shoulder into the pocket of the wave

Dawn patrol: Early morning surf session

Ding: A cut, crack or bump on the surface of the surfboard

Drop-in: Stealing the right of way of another surfer. Also the take-off in a half-pipe on a skateboard

Drop: riding down the wave immediately after the take-off

Duck-dive: Advanced technique to get through a wave with the surfboard

Fish: Surfboard with a specially shaped swallowtail. Tom Curren has made this popular again

Floater: A manoeuvre allowing the surfer to glide over the white water of a breaking wave

Frontside: (to surf on the forehand) Surfing facing the wave

Full deck: Grip deck for both the rear and the front foot

Full suit: Also called a 'Steamer'. A wetsuit with long arms and long legs

Glassy: Smooth water surface resulting from absolutely calm wind conditions

Goofy: Also called 'goofy-foot'. A surfer who surfs with the right foot forward

Green room: See 'Tube'

Grip deck: Rough material fixed on the upper side of the surfboard, as a substitute for wax, to stop one slipping off the board

Grommet: Also called 'Gremmie'. A very young surfer

Groundswell: Strong swell caused by a violent storm far away off the coast

Gun: A big wave board

Hardcore surfer: A dedicated radical surfer

Hollow wave: Wave with a steep and concave face

Hybrid: A mixture of long and shortboard

Impact zone: The point where the lip of the wave meets the surface of the water

Inside rail: The side of the surfboard nearest the wave face. During a tube ride only the inside rail holds the board in the wave

Inside: The end of a wave where it meets reefs or points.

Sitting on the inside – sitting close to the breaking edge of the wave. The surfer on the inside has priority

King tide: Extreme differences in the tide that occurs only on a few days in the year

Late take-off: A difficult start of a ride

where one waits until the wave is extremely steep before standing up

Leash: A cord fixed to the ankle that attaches the board to the surfer

Line-up: The point in the water where the waves break and surfers wait for the wave. Also an orientation point on land as seen from the water

Lip: The front edge of the breaking wave where all the power is concentrated

Localism: Unfriendly behaviour by the locals towards surfers from outside

Longboarder: Surfer who uses a long Malibu board in the classical style

Mushy waves: Waves whipped up by the wind

New school: A new radical way of surfing: aerials, tail-slides, reverse-surfing etc.

North shore: The Mecca for surfers on the north coast of Oahu/Hawaii with many famous surf spots such as Pipeline, Sunset Beach and Waimea Bay

Nose-dive: The tip of the board digs into the water; usually ends up in a wipe-out

Nose: The front of the board

Offshore: When the wind is blowing from the land onto the sea creating a smooth surface on the wave face

Off-the-lip: A manoeuvre whereby a top-turn is made directly onto the lip of a breaking wave

Ollie-hop: An expression borrowed from skateboarders to express a small aerial jump

Onshore: When the wind is blowing from the sea onto the land and creating choppy conditions

Overhead: When the wave is higher than the surfer standing on his board

Peak: Top of a wave; the highest point of a wave. Similarly also a wave breaking to the right and the left (A - frame peak)

Pigdog: Technique enabling a tube to be ridden on the backhand

Pintail: A tapered end of the surfboard

Pipeline: A surfspot on the North Shore in Hawaii with gnarly tubes breaking in shallow water

Pitch: The moment when the lip throws out to form a tube

Plug: An inlay at the tail of the board where the leash is attached

Point break: Where the wave breaks along a headland

Pro surfer: A professional surfer – abbreviated to 'pro'

Pumping: Build up speed by 'pumping' the board up and down on a wave

Quad: A surfboard with four fins

Rails: The edges of the surfboard

Rail saver: A piece of nylon at the end of the leash to protect the board from damage, or to prevent the fingers being squashed when pulling the board behind while diving through a wave

Rash: A skin irritation caused by the sun or rubbing

Re-entry: Also called 'Reo'. "See Off-the-lip"

Rebound: Also called 'Ricochet'. A turn executed on the breaking lip of the wave after a cutback in order to turn back into the 'right' direction

Reef break: Waves that break over reefs

Regular: Also called 'Regular foot'. A surfer who surfs with the left foot forward

Rhino chaser: A large surfboard for big waves

Rocker: The bottom curve of a surfboard

Rookie: A young hot up-and-coming surfer

Secret spot: A 'secret' surfing beach with no surfers in the water

Section: A segment of the wave. To section: Several parts of the wave break down at once. Making it impossible to ride from start to end

Set: A group of waves

Shape: The surfboard form

Shaper: Person who builds surfboards

Shore break: A wave that breaks directly onto the dry sand

Shortboard: A short surfboard about 6 feet long for performance surfing

Slop: Bad, chopped-up waves

Snaking: Competing unfairly or stealing the priority for a wave

Snap: A manoeuvre where the surfer executes a rapid violent turn at the top of the wave wall

Spray: Water thrown or splashed up by a quick turn

Spring suit: A wetsuit with short arms and legs

Square tail: Straight rear end to the surf board. Standard form of the tail.

Stall: A braking or slowing ('stalling') movement in order to allow the tube to catch up

Stringer: A thin strip of wood let into the length of the board to add stability

Sucky waves: Very steep waves that suck up the water from the base of the wave

Surfari: A 'wave hunting' trip

Surf camp: Accommodation that particularly caters for surfers at a good surfing spot

Surf check: Checking the waves from a spot on the beach

Surf session: The time spent in the water surfing

Surf spot: A beach suitable for surfing

Swallow tail: The rear end of a surfboard shaped in the form of a swallow tail

Swell: Waves before they break

Tail slide: Placing pressure on the tail of the board during an extreme turn so that the rear end 'breaks' away

Tail: Rear end of the surfboard

Take-off: The start of a ride

Thruster: A surfboard with three fins positioned at the rear end of the board. One in the middle and one on each side

To backdoor: Taking (or entering) a tube from behind at high speed. The opposite is to 'stall' to get in the tube

To rip: Extreme radical way to surf. 'Ripper' – a very good surfer

Top-to-bottom wave: A wave that breaks directly from the top into the bottom of the wave. Generally this creates a tube

Top-turn: A turn executed on the top edge of a wave

Tube: A tunnel is formed behind the lip of the breaking wave and the rest of the wave. A surfer is able to surf for a short time in this space. The most popular manoeuvre for surfers

Tube suit: A wetsuit with short legs and a sleeveless vest shaped upper part

Wall: The face of a wave that has not yet broken

White water: The foam of a broken wave

Wetshirt: Also called 'Rash guard'. A thin shirt made of Lycra to provide protection from the sun or rashes caused by rubbing the skin

Wetsuit: A surf suit made from Neoprene

Windswell: Weak swell created by winds near the coast (opposite is groundswell)

Wipe-out: To fall off the board

Information

Surfrider Foundation
122 S.El Camino Real No. 67
San Clemente, CA 92672
USA

This is an environmental organisation whose aim is to protect and look after the world's seas, waves and beaches.

Europe
WAVETOURS
Martin Storck & Uli Scherb
Beckstrasse 54
64287 Darmstadt Germany
Phone: +49-6151-4 57 27
Fax: +49-6151-42 50 52
www.wavetours.com

Spain
Ineika Funcentre Fuerteventura
Surf School
Sigi Opitz
Apt. Nr 53 Corralejo
Phone (Fuerte): +34-9-28 53 57 44
Phone (Ger): +49-89-4 31 44 03
Fax (Ger): +49-89-43 65 11 67
Phone (Switzerland):
+41-31-35 28 022
Fax (Switzerland):
+41-31-35 28 174
e-mail: Ineikafun@aol.com
www.ineika.de

Portugal
The Surf Experience
P.O. Box 612, 8600 Lagos, Portugal
Phone: +351 2 82 26 09 64
Fax: +351 2 82 76 72 88
e-mail: surfexperience@clix.pt
www.thesurfexperience.de

Australia
STC The Surf Travel Company
25 Cronullu Plaza
Cronullu Beach, NSW 2230
Phone: +61-2-95 27 47 22
Fax: +61-2-95 27 45 22
www.surftravel.com.au

USA
Electra Bicycle Co.
Benno Baenziger and Jeanno
538 N.Hwy 101
Leucadia, CA 92024
Phone: +1-619-632-7094
Fax: +1-619-632-7829
www.electrabike.com

Fiji
Tavarua Island Resort
Book via: P.O. Box 60159
Santa Barbara, CA 93160
USA
Phone: +1 679-805-686-4551
Fax: +1 679-805-683-6696

Namotu Island
Blue Water Surf Resort
Book via: P.O. Box 980
Coffs Harbour, NSW 2450
Australia
Phone (Aus): +61-1-800-500465

Surf links

www.asplive.com
www.yahoo.com/Recreation/Sports/Surfing
www.eurosurf.tm.fr
www.maui.net/~hookipa/jaws/index.html
magna.com.au/~prfbrown/tubelink. html
www.surfrider.org
www.h30.com

Company

www.byrnesurf.com
www.surfgotcha.com
www.oneill.com
www.reefbrazil.com
www.quiksilver.com

Magazines

www.surfermag.com
www.msp.com.au/tracks

Reports

www.atinternet.fr/lacanausurf
surfcam.com au
www.surfline.com
www.surfrider.org/earth.htm
www.realsurf.com

Travel

www.wavetours.com
www.surftravel.com.au

www.bajasurfadventures.com
www.surfline.com
www.waterwaystravel.com
www.surfingadventures.com
www.ineika.de

Weather

www.fnoc.navy.mil/

Tell us what you think about this book under:
euro_tubes@yahoo.de

Thanks to all those without whose help this book would not have been possible. In alphabetical order:

Benno and Jeano from Electra, Conny Jarosch, The Biarritz Boys, Ecki (ES) Hillebrecht, The Diel Family, Fanatic, The Menges Family, Meyer & Meyer Sports, Heidi Bursch, Jan "Leo" Leopold, Joli Productions, Kuta Lines, Natalie Maag, O'Neill, Pete "Snitzengruben" Longhurst, Quiksilver, Roland "Maurice" Hansky, Sigi "Captain Lobos" Opitz, Stefan "Muli" Müller, The State of Victoria, "Dr. Surf" Thomas Herold, Tony King from STC, Uli and Martin from Wave Tours, Windsurfing Chiemsee

–and anyone we have forgotten to mention.